The *Horse* That Worked For God

and other devotionals for families

Mary Ellen Beachy

Vision
PUBLISHERS

Harrisonburg, Virginia

ISBN-13: 978-1-932676-16-3
ISBN-10: 1-932676-16-7

Printed in the United States of America

Cover Design: Mari Jean Beachy
Editorial Review: Timothy Kennedy, Shannon Latham, John D. Risser, and others
Digital Text entry: Elizabeth B. Burkholder

All scripture taken from the King James Version unless otherwise indicated.

For information regarding special discounts for bulk purchases, please contact:
Vision Publishers Orders at 1-877-488-0901 or write
Vision Publishers at P.O. Box 190, Harrisonburg, VA 22803

For information or comments write to:
Vision Publishers
P.O. Box 190
Harrisonburg, VA 22803
Phone: 877/488-0901
Fax: 540/437-1969
E-mail: orders@vision-publishers.com
www.vision-publishers.com
(see order form in back)

Contents

chapter one

Tell It to Jesus

The Power of Prayer

Moses prayed; his prayer did save
A nation from death and from the grave

Joshua prayed; the sun stood still.
His enemies fell in vale and hill.

Hannah prayed; God gave her a son.
A nation back to the Lord he won.

Solomon for wisdom prayed;
The wisest of mortal men he was made.

Elijah prayed with great desire;
God gave him rain and sent him fire.

Elisha prayed with strong emotion;
He got the mantle and double portion.

Three Hebrews prayed; through flames they trod.
They had as a comrade the Son of God.

Daniel prayed; the lions' claws
Were held by the angel who locked their jaws.

Ten lepers prayed, to the priest were sent.
Glory to God! They were healed as they went.

The thief who prayed, for mercy cried.
He went with Christ to paradise.
The church, she prayed, then got a shock
When Peter answered her prayer with a knock!

Peter prayed, and Dorcas arose
To life again from death's repose.

The disciples kept praying; the Spirit came
With cloven tongues and revival flame!
Conviction filled the hearts of men;
Three thousand souls were born again!

When Christians pray as they prayed of yore,
With living faith for souls implore,
In one accord united stand,
Revival fires shall sweep the land!
And sinners shall converted be
And all the world God's glory see!

—Author Unknown

Prayers in Romania

David was a cheerful eight-year-old lad with brown eyes and brown hair. He lived at the Nathanael Christian Orphanage in Romania. He was loved and happy. Best of all, he was taught about Jesus, the One who loves all children from every land.

One day David was taken to the hospital for some minor surgery. He lay on the operating table, waiting for the doctor. A few seconds before the anesthesia was given to him, David remembered something and said, "Sir, doctor, please don't start the surgery!"

The doctor kindly asked, "Why, what happened, David?"

David replied, "Sir, I forgot to pray to Jesus to help you with the surgery!"

All the people in the operating room fell silent as David, the little boy from the orphanage, who was born in a bad neighborhood but was adopted by the large and loving family of God, began to pray loudly and fervently. When he said, "Amen," there was silence. No one said a word, but there were tears in the eyes of all the people who were dressed in white.

The surgery was successful, and today David is healthy. That day all of the hospital personnel learned what the children at the orphanage were being taught. He helped many people learn a lesson about prayer. These people then reached out and taught many more. Praise the Lord!

Florica was a girl at the same orphanage. Florica grew up in a poverty-stricken Gypsy family. When she visited her home one day, Florica told her family about God. She explained the way of salvation to them and told them how she prayed before eating and before going to bed. A neighbor lady also came over to listen to Florica tell the story of salvation.

The witness of these children and others from Nathanael Christian Orphanage spreads to other orphanages and to churches where they share in song.

Story taken from Christian Aid Ministries newsletter, December 1996. Used by permission.

read and consider...

Why was it important for David to pray before the surgery? What did Florica share with her family about prayer?

Read Isaiah 11:6 and Luke 18:15–17.
Matthew 21:15, 16: "And when the chief priests and the scribes saw the wonderful things that he did, and the children crying in the temple, and saying, Hosanna to the son of David; they were sore displeased, and said unto him, Hearest thou what these say? And Jesus saith unto them, Yea; have ye never read, Out of the mouth of babes and sucklings thou hast perfected praise?"

Empty Bowls

The big, black rice pot was cold and empty. There was no more nice white rice to cook and eat. What would Amy Carmichael and her orphan girls do? Not only was the rice gone, there was no money to buy more.

Amy, a missionary in India for many years, had learned to depend totally on God for everything. Daily she studied God's Word to know God better and to know His will for her family of orphans.

While they were still at prayer, a messenger arrived. He handed Amy an envelope. Inside she found one hundred rupees. The prayer meeting turned into a praise meeting. What a blessing it was that God heard and answered their prayers for rice!

A little playmate from the village was watching. She saw the hungry girls and she heard them pray. She saw how God sent them the money. She was deeply impressed by the Christian's powerful God!

Sometime later, Amy and her family were able to purchase a farm. Now they could raise their own rice and other foods. Their first rice seedlings grew nicely. Amy and the girls rejoiced to see the field spread out, a refreshing sheet of green. But then the weather turned hot and dry for a few days. Hosts of wiggly caterpillars hatched out in the hot sun. There were so many caterpillars that the man in charge of the rice fields knew the crop could be ruined. He told Amy, the workers, and the children about the serious caterpillar problem. He begged them to pray that God would protect their rice. Even the small children understood, and they all prayed fervently for God to save the rice.

Two days later, when the farmer again checked the rice fields, a most wonderful sight met his worried eyes. White cattle egrets (small white herons) were marching up and down the green rows of rice. They were greedily feasting on the juicy caterpillars. The rice field was saved!

In much of the surrounding countryside the horrible caterpillars completely destroyed the rice fields. But Amy and her children again had a praise meeting. Their faith was strengthened. Truly God did care! He loved them! He heard and answered their prayers!

read and consider...

What did Amy do to know God's will?
How did God save the rice crop from the caterpillars?
Is anything too hard for God?

Read: Jeremiah 32:17, 27 and Malachi 3:10.
Psalm 55:17: "Evening, and morning, and at noon, will I pray, and cry aloud; and he shall hear my voice."

The Pocket That Answered Prayer

"Oh, God," Mosa prayed, "I need help. How will I ever be able to pay the 10 million lei in overdue bills for our apartment? How can I possibly provide for my family? I don't have the money for the bills, Lord. Please, can you help us?"

It was the summer of 2003, and life in Romania was not easy. Food, work, and clothing were in short supply for Mosa and his family. So they were extremely grateful when a Christian Aid Ministry worker, Neko Catso, drove to their house with a food parcel and a clothing parcel. This was like a breath of cool air and hope on a stifling summer day. Mosa thought that here might be an answer to his prayer for money.

"I cannot pay the back rent for my apartment, I need ten million lei. Can you help me?" Mosa asked Neko.

The driver regretfully said, "I can't help now; our summer program is not activated yet. I don't have funds to share. Maybe later in the fall we can help you."

Mosa took the food and clothing parcel and went into his house. He felt God was not answering his prayer. He was disappointed and sad as he opened the clothing parcel. Absentmindedly he pulled out the clothing and thought about which one would fit each child. He heard a rustle in one of the garments. He looked closer; yes, there was a pocket. What could be inside? He reached a work-worn hand into the pocket and pulled out a wad of money. It was not 20, 50, or 100 dollars—it was 300 dollars! Mosa stared in amazement! How could this be? He needed 10 million lei, and the 300 dollars was just right, for ten million lei is equivalent to 298 dollars.

Mosa fell on his knees in thanksgiving. God *had* heard his cry for help!

Shared by Nathan Bange at Christian Aid Ministries Open House, 2003.
Used by permission.

read and consider...

When in need, where do we go for help?
Does God always answer our prayers in the way we think He
    should?

Read Psalm 23:1 and John 14:1, 2
Philippians 4:19: "But my God shall supply all your need according to his riches in glory by Christ Jesus."

Our Powerful God

Prayer makes the darkest cloud withdraw;
Prayer climbs the ladder Jacob saw,
Gives exercise to faith and love,
Brings every blessing from above.

Restraining prayer, we cease to fight;
Prayer makes the Christian's armor bright;
And Satan trembles when he sees
The weakest saint upon his knees.

—William Cowper

In 1839 the sultan (a ruler of a Muslim country) of Turkey decreed that not one Christian should remain in his empire any longer. When Dr. William Goodell, an American missionary to Turkey, heard the sultan's orders, he was greatly disturbed.

He went to his friend and coworker, Dr. Cyrus Hamlin, with the news that they must leave Turkey. "The American consul and the British ambassador say it is no use to meet with this violent and vindictive monarch; it would only antagonize him. We will have to leave Turkey," Dr. William sadly stated.

To this Dr. Hamlin replied, "Our great God, the sultan of the universe can, in answer to prayer, change the decree of the Sultan of Turkey. Let us not lose heart, but fervently pray."

The men gave themselves to prayer. They beseeched the Lord to allow them to continue His work in Turkey. The next day the Sultan of Turkey died! His decree was never executed.

read and consider...

Is anything too hard for God?
What should we do before we make any big decision?

Read: Daniel 4:17 and Proverbs 21:1.
Luke 18:1: "Men ought always to pray, and not to faint."

The Hot Pocket

Starla smiled with satisfaction as she viewed her work, stacks and stacks of precisely typed Bible stories. All of the stories had finally been translated and typed into French Creole. A Haitian couple had been at Life Ministries to work on the translating. Now, after many months of work, the project was ready to send to the print shop. All except one thing, one major thing. Ten thousand dollars were needed to get the printing done!

Dan, Starla's friend from the print shop, stopped in at eight o'clock that morning. He knew the Bible story translating project was nearing completion.

"Is the project for Haiti ready to send to the press?" he asked Starla.

"Yes, it is all completed," Starla said, "but we don't have the funds to get it printed now."

Lester walked in at that moment. "We won't send this project with you until we have the ten thousand dollars we need to get it printed," he stated.

"That is no problem," Dan responded. "We are happy to start on the printing, and you can pay us, Les, whenever the money comes in."

"No," Lester replied, "I will not send it with you until we have the funds. It's not wise to borrow the money. Some day God will make a way. I will give you a call when I want you to pick it up."

Lester called his family and the staff at Life Ministries together. He presented the need for ten thousand dollars for the Bible storybooks for Haiti. He proposed they spend the day in prayer and fasting. Right then they had a prayer meeting. At noon, Lester, his wife Betty, and others fasted and prayed, imploring almighty God to meet their needs.

At one-thirty that afternoon the phone rang in Lester's office. A man asked, "Do you need ten thousand dollars?"

"Do we need ten thousand dollars?!" Lester exclaimed. "Yes, yes indeed we do. We were praying for that VERY amount this VERY day!"

"It's like this," the man said. "I have ten thousand dollars I need to give to you. I will bring it in. At lunch time today it seemed like my wallet just burned in my pocket. I didn't know what was going on. I got my wallet out and opened it. I found a check that I made out to you three weeks ago that I forgot to send. The amount is ten thousand dollars."

Lester went running to find Betty. "God answered our prayer already," he rejoiced. "God answered our prayer this very day while we were fasting and praying. God is so good. God did it!"

Another prayer meeting was held at Life Ministries that day, a meeting of praise and thanksgiving to God for hearing and answering their prayer.

Lester promptly called Dan to come and pick up the Bible stories. Dan walked in the door and said incredulously, "What! Do you mean you have the money now?"

Why is God honored when His children pray?

Do you pray about your needs?

Who made the man feel like his wallet was hot in his pocket?

Read Daniel 9:3, 4, 20, 22.

1 Thessalonians 5:17: "Pray without ceasing."

God loves to hear His children praying,

God delights to answer prayer.

A Praying Man and an Obedient Ship

"Unless almighty God has mercy on us, there is no hope," shouted the captain. "I have never seen a wilder sea!"

The *Dumfries*, the ship Hudson Taylor had boarded to sail to China, tossed and pitched on the wild ocean. The sea was white with foam. Waves towered above the ship on either side. Hudson felt sick as he watched the sun set over the stormy sea. He thought: *Tomorrow the sun will rise but unless the Lord helps us through, only broken timbers will be left of the* Dumfries.

As Hudson thought of his family, tears came to his eyes. Was his goal of reaching the lost in China to be dashed to pieces in a watery grave? A verse from Psalm 50 came to his mind. "Call upon me in the day of trouble: I will deliver you." Hudson bowed his head and earnestly prayed that God would spare their lives.

A bright moon arose. The men on the ship could plainly see land. Hudson doubted that lifeboats could survive on the raging sea.

The seasoned captain mocked Hudson: "No, we can't live for more than half an hour. What of your call to work for God in China now?"

Hudson replied, "I am glad to be on board. I still expect to reach China. If we never make it, my Master will say it was well that I was seeking to obey His will and commands."

Why was Hudson Taylor willing to leave home and risk his life to travel halfway around the world to China on September 19, 1835?

Before Hudson was born, his parents had prayed, *"Lord, if you give us a son, grant that he may work for you in China."*

Hudson's parents rejoiced when he gave his heart and life to God. They rejoiced when he prepared for mission work. But the parting tore at their heart strings! Mother and son wondered if they would ever meet again in this life.

Yes, Hudson was bravely sailing to China with the message of truth and life, to a land where millions were dying without hope.

Now the storm-tossed ship drifted toward the rocks. The captain tried desperately to turn back out to sea but could not. Soon they were only two ship lengths from the rocks. Just then, the wind changed direction, and the storm gradually blew itself out! Hudson rejoiced to see the morning. How he thanked the Lord. Every answer to prayer strengthened his faith in God almighty.

God, who can calm the raging seas, can also send a wind if need be. Later on the same voyage, there was no breeze at all. Grave danger threatened again, for the current began to carry them toward New Guinea. The shore there was perilous with sunken reefs, and the island also was unsafe, for it was the home of painted head hunters!

"We've done everything we can," said the captain to Hudson. "We will just have to wait and see the outcome."

"No, there is one thing we have not done," stated Hudson. "Four of us on this ship are Christians. We must pray and ask the Lord to send us a breeze. He can send it NOW, just as easily as at sunset."

How fervently the four prayed! Hudson felt a peace that God would answer. He went on deck and told the first officer to let down the mainsail. "We've been asking God to send a wind, and it is coming. There is not a moment to lose!"

The first officer mocked, "I would rather see a wind than hear of one!"

Even as they spoke the men glanced upward. The corner of the sail was beginning to flutter in the coming breeze! The mainsail came down, and in a few minutes they were sailing away from the dangerous shore and the savages!

And on March 1, 1854, Hudson saw the shores of the mysterious land of China.

read and consider...

Why did Hudson Taylor want to sail to China?
How did his parents feel about it?

Read: Acts 27:14–25.
Isaiah 6:8: "Also I heard the voice of the Lord, saying, Whom shall I send, and who will go for us? Then said I, Here am I; send me."

Mother's Secret

A dear friend sent me this lovely story she found in an old book from the 1800's.

● ● ● ● ● ● ● ● ●

"Mother," said a little ten-year-old girl, "I want to know the secret of your going into the woods every morning and every evening."

Their cottage was a very little one, and when this good mother wanted to be alone to pray, she went into the nearby woods.

"Why do you ask this question, my dear?" said the mother.

"Because I think you must go there to see somebody you love very much."

"What makes you think so?" asked her mother.

"Because I always notice that when you come back, you seem happier than when you went," the little girl replied.

"Well, suppose I do go there to see a friend that I love very much, and that after meeting Him and talking with Him, I feel happier than before. Why should you wish to know anything more about it?"

"Because, Mother," the little girl said, "I should like to go with you, and perhaps it would make me happier too."

"Well, my dear child, when I leave you in the morning and in the evening and go into the woods, I go to meet my blessed Savior and pray to Him. And when I come away, I feel that He is with me; and the thought of His presence is a help and a comfort to me all day."

"Oh, that's the secret of it, is it?" said the child. "Then please, always let me go with you when you go, then perhaps the blessed Savior will be with me, too, to help and comfort me."

read and consider...

Do you have a special place where you go to talk with God? Why did the mother in this story love to pray in the woods?

Read: 1 Peter 5:7 and Psalm 55:22.
Philippians 4:6, 7: "Be careful for nothing; but in everything by prayer and supplication with thanksgiving let your requests be made known unto God. And the peace of God, which passeth all understanding, shall keep your hearts and minds through Christ Jesus."

chapter two

Great Men and Women of God

Great men and women of God

Are not in need of our praise.

We are in need of getting to know them!

Beautiful Feet

Hudson Taylor spent many years serving God in China. When he sailed from England to China in 1853, there were no airplanes. There were no roads leading to the countless villages of China where many, many people needed to hear about Jesus, people who were dying and going to a Christless grave. To reach these people, Hudson Taylor walked.

When Hudson Taylor was an old man, he was still walking—walking to share the news of Jesus. His feet were calloused. Those big, thick calluses on his feet made it painful for him to walk. Still he kept walking till he died. He wanted to tell more and more lost souls of the wonderful news of Jesus' love.

Hudson's wife became too old and weak to accompany him on his long walks for Jesus.

Way back in the interior of China where they lived, she anxiously waited in the twilight for her husband to come home. When he finally reached home, he was utterly weary, worn out from the hot sun, thirsty, and tired. His feet ached.

His faithful companion hurried to get an old tin wash basin and fill it with warm water heated on their stove. She got down on her old knees before her noble husband. Tenderly, lovingly, she washed his calloused and knobby old feet with her tired hands. She gently massaged them while he told her where he had been for Jesus that day. He told her of the lady with a large open sore on her leg whom he had shown the way to heaven, of the demon possessed person he prayed for, and of the village where half of the people were blind or going blind with tra-choma, a disease in the eyes. He spoke to them of the great healer, Jesus, who came to give sight to the blind.

Finally, his wife had done her utmost to ease the pain in his tired feet, feet that were wearing out for Jesus. Then she looked affectionately at her faithful husband and said, "I love the way your face shines for Jesus, Hudson. But your feet are beautiful too. For our Lord said, 'How beautiful upon the mountains are the feet of him that bringeth good tidings, that publisheth peace; that bringeth good tidings of good, that publisheth salvation.' "

They prayed together and retired for the night with peace and joy in their hearts. They were giving their best, their all for Jesus.

In 1905, at the age of 73 years, Hudson Taylor died in Changsha. He was buried in China among the people he dearly loved.

read and consider...

The children's song says, "Oh be careful little feet where you go. . . ."
Where are your feet taking you each day? Is the Lord pleased with the places you go?
Why did Hudson keep walking with the good news in his old age?

Read Isaiah 52:7 and Psalm 121:7, 8.
Numbers 6:24–26: "The LORD bless thee, and keep thee; the LORD make his face shine upon thee, and be gracious unto thee; the LORD lift up his countenance upon thee, and give thee peace."

Missionary to the Indians

If you had been born in one of the American colonies in the 1700's, to whom could you be a missionary? Did you say the Indians? That is what David Brainard did. David was born in 1718 and died in 1747. He began serving the Indians in his youth, giving his whole life in service to Jesus Christ.

Why would a young man give up all the comforts of home and all he had to live in the wilderness with savage Indians?

David was gripped by the doom of the savages who were dying without Christ. He knew few ministers would volunteer to work with the Indians. He wanted to demonstrate his willingness to suffer and die for Christ, so he battled grave illness and opposition to live out his grreat passion to serve and glorify God.

Discouragement and loneliness knocked at David's door. He often felt his labors were not bearing much fruit for God. But he kept on preaching and praying. He loved the solitude and quietness of nature. He loved to be all alone in the woods where he felt close to God. He cried out to God on behalf of the Indians and as he wrestled in prayer, he found strength from God.

Some of the Delaware Indians were fearful to turn to God. They said, "If we forsake our religion, we will be poisoned by the medicine man."

"Don't be afraid," David pleaded. "I challenge the powers of darkness to do their worst upon me first!" Nothing happened. "See," rejoiced David, "the powwows have not poisoned or bewitched me. My God is most powerful!"

In Crossweeksung (now Crosswicks), New Jersey, David was greatly heartened when the Delaware Indians received his message. Day by day, more Indians came through the forest to hear the Word of God.

On August 25, 1745, about 95 Indians came to the service. That day David baptized 15 adults and 10 young people. His heart was filled with joy and thankfulness to God. One old man who loved Indian dances voluntarily surrendered the rattles he used to make music. The Indians promptly destroyed their objects of pagan worship.

What a difference it makes when the Lord comes into the hearts of lost sinners! David saw old men and women who had been drunken wretches for many years become convicted of their sins and find hope in Christ. God was destroying the kingdom of darkness among the Indians. David rejoiced to see a growing sensitivity and soul-searching among them.

read and consider...

Why was David willing to give up the comforts of home to be a missionary to the Indians?

Why were some of the Delaware Indians afraid to come to God?

Read I John 3:8, 9, 16.

1 John 4:4: "Ye are of God, little children, and have overcome them: because greater is he that is in you, than he that is in the world."

Lord, Send Me

Jonathan Goforth, a poor Canadian farm boy, was born on February 2, 1859. He answered God's call to share His love with the vast multitudes of people in China. Jonathan and his wife Rosalind gave nearly 50 years of their lives in service to that needy nation. They braved disaster, danger, and disease so the Chinese could find the Savior.

Little did they know what that decision would cost. By the time they had been in China three and one half years, two of their three children had died. God gave them eleven children; five of them were buried in China.

During the terrible violence and unrest of the Boxer Rebellion, the Goforths fled for their lives, narrowly escaping death. Thousands of Chinese Christians and over 250 foreign missionaries were killed.

The Goforths were poor and hungry. They were sometimes spat upon. Once, Jonathan was beaten. Yet through all the hardships, God was their constant rock and defender.

Jonathan was a man of great self discipline. Even before he came to Christ, he gave up dancing, card playing, and reading questionable literature. He felt they wasted his time, time that could be spent in worthwhile projects. After he came to the Lord, Jonathan viewed these as hindrances of spiritual power. His utmost goal in life was to do the will of his Father.

In his youth, Jonathan had decided to serve God by becoming a pastor. But one night that goal changed as he listened spellbound to an elderly missionary to Formosa.

Dr. Mackay preached a lively sermon. Toward the end of his message his voice grew quiet. "I have traveled from one end of Canada to the other in the past two years," he said, "trying to find a young man to work with me in my mission. I cannot find a man; why has no one caught the vision? Must I go back alone? Soon I will die and be buried on some lonely Formosa hillside. That is no catastrophe. But a great sadness overcomes me that no man has heard the call to carry on the work which God helped me to begin."

Jonathan felt overwhelmed with shame. He was planning to serve God in his homeland, not in a foreign country. Isaiah 6:8 came to his mind: "Whom shall I send, and who will go for us?" In his heart he felt the call of God on his life. He knew God was calling him to be a missionary to a foreign land where no one had ever preached the gospel, and he was willing to go.

In the meantime, Jonathan's time was consumed with studies and work at the Toronto mission. He was too poor at times to buy even a postage stamp. His best suit was worn and tattered. He needed a better one and earnestly prayed about it.

One day as he walked past a tailor shop, the owner called out, "Say, Goforth, come in, you are the very man I am looking for." The tailor brought out a suit of the best quality and told Jonathan to try it on.

Jonathan objected, "I cannot afford this!" The man insisted. Jonathan tried the suit and it fit perfectly.

"Now," said the tailor, "it's yours unless you are too proud to accept it. A customer ordered this suit, but was not satisfied and left it on my hands."

Jonathan walked out with the new suit. It was a wonderful answer to prayer. How he thanked God!

(to be continued)

read and consider...

What were some of the hardships Jonathan and Rosalind faced in China?

What did he do when he needed a new suit?

Read: Jeremiah 33:3 and Psalm 119:9.

Proverbs 8:34, 35: "Blessed is the man that heareth me, watching daily at my gates, waiting at the posts of my doors. For whoso findeth me findeth life, and shall obtain favor of the Lord."

Missionaries Need Intercessors

The more Jonathan Goforth studied and learned about China, the more convinced he became that China was the place he should serve as a missionary. He felt there was no other place where so many people had never heard about Jesus.

While working at the Toronto Mission Union, he met Rosalind Bell Smith, a talented girl from a wealthy home. Jonathan was attracted by her sincerity and commitment to God. Later, when Jonathan proposed, he seriously asked, "Will you join your life with mine for China?"

Rosalind replied, "Oh, Jonathan, of course I will."

Jonathan knew their life would be filled with hardships and challenges. Yet, together with God, the future looked bright. Their plans were laid to sail to China.

* * * * * * * *

Jonathan sat with his head in his hands. "Rosalind," he said, "unless the Lord works a miracle for me with this language, I fear I shall be a total failure as a missionary. I study hard, but for me this language is extremely difficult. I wonder if I am even capable of learning Chinese."

When it was Jonathan's turn to read the Bible to the natives, they would say, "We don't understand you." He dreaded when it was his turn to preach; he knew even the most patient Chinese could hardly figure out what he said.

One day as Jonathan was walking to chapel he earnestly prayed, "God, unlock the keys of this language to me. Oh God, you know I long to win souls. Lord, have mercy and help me."

On that memorable day, when it was his turn to preach, everything he had studied seemed to come into focus. The Chinese sat up and listened and told him, "Keep on talking!"

That breakthrough was a source of great encouragement. It gave him confidence that God would help him master the language.

Two months later a letter from a former roommate said that one evening after supper a group of students got together to pray for Goforth. Everyone at that prayer meeting clearly felt God's presence and power. "How do our prayers help you?" the friend wrote.

Jonathan looked at the dates. "Rosalind," he excitedly called, "they were praying for me in Canada on the evening when I could finally speak the language!"

read and consider...

What can you do to help you remember to pray for missionaries? How about making a missionary prayer list?

Read Acts 1:8 and Luke 10:2.
1 Thessalonians 5:24, 25: "Faithful is he that calleth you, who also will do it. Brethren pray for us."

Children Are a Gift From God

A large crowd of men was toiling up the hill on their way to the temple of the goddess. The Chinese believed this goddess had the power to give a male baby to men who sacrificed to her. It was an honor and a point of great pride to a Chinese family to have a son. Many men came, some from hundreds of miles away, to implore the goddess for a son.

Jonathan and a Chinese Christian were preaching nearby. Mr. Chou called out to the crowd, "You are worshiping a goddess who has no power to give you a son. The Christian's God is the one with power. Their God restored my eyesight and opened the eyes of my sin-darkened soul. I used to be a wicked man, as you know. Now I want to do good because my heart is filled with the love of God."

Jonathan took his turn preaching. "I have nine brothers and one sister. My wife has nine brothers and three sisters. No one from our land ever heard of this goddess, and yet our two families have a total of nineteen sons. It is the true God from heaven who gives sons and daughters to us." Jonathan held up his big, black Bible. "God's holy book tells me this. Children are a gift from the living God. You will have a son if it is in the will of God. It has absolutely nothing to do with this goddess or any sacrifice you offer to her."

The mayor of the town had been leading the large procession. He stopped to hear what the men were saying. He turned to the crowd, "Go on if you please. I will stop to hear more about this God."

"I want to become a Christian," the mayor said three hours later. "I will wait for God to give me a son." This mayor went on to become a dedicated student of the Word of God. He memorized the four gospels and preached every chance that came his way.

Jonathan rejoiced greatly that this new Chinese Christian was a man of courage and leadership. Many years later, in 1909, Jonathan was visiting friends in London. He was taken to visit an invalid lady who told him she had once had a great burden to pray for Goforth. She had heard of his plans for meetings in Manchuria, and she had beseeched heaven's throne to bless Goforth's ministry. She had recorded three dates when she sensed a special power in prayer.

Jonathan recalled those dates as the very days when he had witnessed God mightily at work

---

Resources: *Jonathan Goforth* by Rosalind Goforth.
An Open Door in China, Janet and Geoff Benge, 2001, by YMAM.

read and consider...

Children are a gift from_____.
What great ministry can invalids have?

Read Psalm 128.
Matthew 6:33: "But seek ye first the kingdom of God, and his righteousness; and all these things shall be added unto you."

David Livingstone, the Fearless Explorer

How would you like to travel by foot through the jungles of Africa? You could take an old muzzle loader shotgun and hire some local Africans to carry your supplies. Or would you feel more secure traveling by oxcart? Nightfall finds you camping around a blazing campfire, sleeping beneath stars that hang so low you'd feel you could reach out and touch them.

One hundred and fifty years ago, the sun beat down unmercifully on a small band of men who were exploring the interior of Africa on foot and by oxcart. Their leader, Dr. David Livingstone, was ever watchful and alert. He paused to examine blooming orchids and studied teeming ant hills. Little escaped his watchful eye. One day, he and his African men suddenly stiffened with fright. Up ahead on the trail, they saw a huge black rhinoceros charging toward them. There was no place to hide! When the rhino was nearly upon them, it swerved aside. Was it, like the Africans, dumbfounded by its first sight of a white man? Or had a guardian angel blocked its path?

David Livingstone was born in Scotland on March 19, 1813. After medical training, he traveled to Africa. Livingstone was a scientist, physician, missionary, and a courageous explorer. He was also the first white man to travel into the vast African interior. The land was full of wild beasts. Livingstone met hostile slave traders, wary natives, and teeming clouds of mosquitoes. He suffered from malaria several times. He narrowly escaped death—threatened by elephants, attacked by a lion, and endangered by men's spears. He once said, "We seem immortal, till our work is done."

After four years in Africa, Dr. Livingstone married Mary Moffat, a fellow missionary's daughter. The first few years of marriage, they worked together, teaching the natives and raising a family. Their marriage was marked by a mutual love and respect, and later they endured lengthy separations. Dr. Livingstone took his family along on short exploratory trips, determined to find a healthy location for inland missions. But the malaria and rough travel of the interior were too much for Mary and David's children. So Livingstone sent his family back to England while he continued his explorations.

One day the doctor's contrary ox flung him into a murky river. Twenty of his African men dived simultaneously into the water to rescue him. When he and all the men emerged, dripping wet and safe, their joy was unbounded. David said, "I would rather die than see my men sold into slavery." Is it any wonder his men had an extraordinary regard and respect for their leader?

Native friends told the explorer about a mysterious smoke that thunders. As he and his men traced the source of the Zambezi River, they saw clouds of mist and vapor on the horizon. They were still ten miles away, but as they traveled nearer, they heard the thundering roar of rushing water. Africa's largest waterfalls was just ahead. Dr. Livingstone stood in awe as he watched the mighty waters plummet 360 feet into the Zambezi River. The first European to see this majestic sight, Livingstone named the falls Victoria Falls, after Queen Victoria of England. On a little tree, on a nearby island, David carved his initials and the year, 1855. Livingstone wrote, "Scenes so lovely must be gazed upon by angels in their flight." Today, Victoria Falls is considered one of the seven natural wonders of the world.

(to be continued)

read and consider...

Why are missionaries willing to brave many dangers to bring the Gospel to lost mankind?

What were some of the dangers Dr. Livingstone faced?

Read: Jeremiah 1:7, 8 and Acts 4:12.

2 Corinthians 5:15: "And that he died for all, that they which live should not henceforth live unto themselves, but unto him which died for them, and rose again."

Determined David

A friend of Dr. Livingstone's once said, "Fire, water or stone wall will not stop David. He traveled 29,000 weary miles in Africa, adding about a million square miles to the then-known map of the world."

Dr. Livingstone aptly said, "No great result is ever attained without patient, long continued effort." His hardships were daily and many: scarcity of food, bouts of fever, insufficient medicines, continued drenchings, exhausting heat, and endless toil. "So many difficulties have been put in my way," he wrote, "I'm doubting whether God is with me, yet, I shall not begrudge my hunger and toils if the good Lord permits me to put a stop to the enormous evils of the inland slave trade."

The explorer was consumed with his goal of opening the interior of Africa for commerce and Christianity. He was sorely burdened with the awful horrors of the slave trade, which he saw on every hand. He wrote extensive books, letters, and journals to expose this evil. Eventually, his writings were influential in stamping out slavery.

Dr. Livingstone's explorations won him great honor and fame. On his two trips back to England, he was given a hero's welcome. People from many countries eagerly followed the news of his explorations in the Dark Continent. And then, suddenly, the news stopped. Rumors spread that Dr. Livingstone was dead. An American newspaper company, the *New York Herald*, decided to find him. A reporter named Henry Stanley was commissioned to spend any amount of money and time to find Dr. Livingstone, dead or alive.

Stanley searched Africa for months. Finally, the reporter found the physician very ill, bed-ridden in a village called Ujiji. Stanley met the missionary with the now famous words, "Dr. Livingstone, I presume." Stanley was the first white man David had spoken with in six years. Stanley shared his ample supplies of food and medicines, and the good doctor's health was restored.

Livingstone wanted to make one more journey to find the hidden fountains—the source of the Nile River. He was certain that it would open up a passage for missionaries and traders to the interior of Africa. After many weeks of travel, the doctor had to stop. A new attack of fever had left him too weak to go on. His men laid him on a crude bed in a small African hut. The next morning they found him kneeling beside his bed. He had died while praying for the Africans he so dearly loved.

Dr. David Livingstone unselfishly gave 30 years of his life for the betterment of the African people.

His faithful men carried his body to the coast. From there, it was taken to London and buried in Westminster Abbey. If you were to visit the site, you would find a headstone that reads, in part, "Brought by faithful hands over land and sea, Here Rests David Livingstone, Missionary Traveler, Philanthropist. Born March 19, 1813, at Blantyre, Lanarkshire. Died May 4th, 1873, at Chitambo's Village, Ilala."

read and consider...

What was the fever Dr. Livingstone suffered from so often?
What beautiful thing was he doing when God called him home?

Read 2 Corinthians 4:16-18.
Philippians 1:21: "For to me to live is Christ, and to die is gain."

Dr. Ida Scudder

Ida Scudder was born in India. Both her father and grandfather had been missionaries in India. But Ida did not want to be a missionary. One night the Lord spoke to her in a vivid, dramatic way about the need for women doctors in India. Ida at last yielded her stubborn will to the will of God.

She served faithfully as a medical missionary in India for 50 years.

Ida's days were full and busy. Her journal entry on November 24, 1909, read: *Such a full day! One hundred and twenty-two patients in Gudiyattam and one hundred and eight on the way, and I could have treated many more if there had been time. My heart was made sad by the need.*[1]

When Ida turned 80 years old, her friends gave her a gala celebration. She was treated like royalty all day. She longed for another 80 years to serve the people of India.

It was this smiling, white-haired woman who created Asia's greatest medical center in Vellore, India. She was asked, "Don't you feel a great satisfaction in seeing all this that you accomplished and remembering how it started?"

"Oh, yes, yes," she fervently replied, "God has been very good to me." She had no pride in her accomplishments, only gratitude to God.

As the years passed, Ida continued to get up at 5:30 every morning. She worked an hour or more in her beautiful garden after breakfast. In her sixties her health and vitality were such that she played tennis with those a quarter her age and often won the game. At 85 she accepted a niece's invitation to go on an elephant trek into the jungle. It was an event she talked about with guests for months to come.

Though Ida wanted to serve longer, it was the will of her Father to call her home on May 24, 1960.

The superintendent of the hospital, an Indian man, gave the eulogy at her funeral. Tears streamed down his cheeks as he said, "Only those who can see the invisible can achieve the impossible. Dr. Ida Scudder has achieved the impossible through her close touch with God, through her faith."

Thousands of people in India and across the world were healed and inspired by the touch of this amazing doctor.

Since 1819, when her grandfather became the first medical missionary from the United States to India, over 30 members of the Scudder family gave a total of nearly 1,000 years to missionary service in that country of vast needs.

(to be continued)

---

1. Resource: *Dr. Ida: Passing on the Torch of Life,* Dorothy Clarke Wilson. New York: Friendship Press, 1976, page 129.

Someday your time on earth will be over. What will people
remember about you?

What did Dr. Ida do for the Lord?

Want to learn more about Dr. Ida? Read: *Ida Scudder: Healing
Bodies and Touching Hearts*, Janet and Geof Benge.
Dr. Ida by Dorothy Clarke Wilson.

Read: Matthew 6:19, 21.

Matthew 7:21: "Not every one that saith unto me, Lord, Lord,
shall enter into the kingdom of heaven; but he that doeth
the will of my Father which is in heaven."

When in need pray and pray.
When in sunshine pray and pray.
Always, in every situation,
Remember to pray and pray!

Bumpy Rides

"Lord," Dr. Ida prayed, "You know I feel called to hold weekly roadside medical clinics for the poor country folk, but the bumpy bandy ride, a two-wheeled oxcart, is so slow and tiring for the hundreds of miles I cover. Lord, could you provide a better way to reach more people for your name's sake?"

Then, one day Dr. Ida received an exciting letter. A supporter from the United States was sending her a 1909 Peugeot motorcar. When the car came, she would be able to visit remote villages much faster!

Ida had driven automobiles several times when she was in the United States. She had never seen a motorcar in or around Vellore, India, where her hospital was. What would the natives think of an animal-less carriage?

Many days later the car had arrived. A man was finally found who knew how to assemble it. Ida's driver had taken some practice runs and was thrilled with the machine. The first time they left for a roadside clinic, Ida breathed a prayer for safety. The one cylinder, French-made Puegeot chugged its way loudly down the rough, rutted roads. Ida had to tell her driver to slow down many times.

The motorcar frightened people along the way. A group of field workers walking along the road heard them coming and shrieked, "The devil is coming! The devil is coming!" In terror they fled into the field.

Ida had the car stopped and ran into the field after the men. "We will not harm you," she called. "I am the doctor who comes to help you each week."

Alas, the men kept on running. One yelled back over his shoulder, "Look how it breathes smoke; it is the devil. An animal-less cart is bad, bad magic."

Ida was not greatly discouraged. At first they had to stop the car a distance from each clinic so the people were not frightened away. But gradually the people became accustomed to the strange automobile.

The gift of the Peugeot enabled Dr. Ida to cover many more miles in a day. Now Ida could treat over three hundred people daily at the roadside clinics.

Ida thanked God for answering her prayer for better transportation so that she could touch more poor country people who needed help physically and spiritually.

(to be continued)

read and consider...

Why did Dr. Ida pray for better transportation?
Why did the car frighten the natives so badly?
What can you give to help a missionary?

Read Philippians 4:6, 7 and Philippians 4:19.
Luke 18:1: "Men ought always to pray, and not to faint."

Boys' Ears and a Bull's Ear

All of Dr. Ida's days were unusual. She never knew what a day would hold, but she had great faith that God held her and her days in the palm of His hand.

A little lad was brought into her dispensary as naked as the day he was born. He complained, "There is a stone in my ear."

Dr. Ida was shocked to see a stone, a large one, that had been pushed deep into his ear canal by another little boy.

Ida patted the lad on his small bony shoulder. "It will hurt when I remove the stone," she frankly told him, "but you are a strong boy; you will be brave for me."

He was brave, never wincing throughout the painful ordeal. He left the dispensary gratefully.

The next day Ida felt a soft tug on her dress. The same little lad was back again, holding another small boy by the hand.

"Here is another boy with a stone in his ear," he said.

The new patient was a tiny fellow, speechless with fright. But while Dr. Ida worked on his ear, his friend stood close beside him. He comforted and reassured him by saying, "Don't be afraid. She won't hurt you any more than she has to."

When the stone was removed, the two little lads, dressed only in nature's clothing, scampered gratefully away, but not before they each dropped a small coin (about a sixth of a cent), in the charity box.

Ida smiled as she watched them run off. The words of Jesus echoed in her ears, "Let the little children come to me. . . ."

Not everyone wanted Dr. Ida's help. The large, needy village of Lathery closed its doors to her. Week after week she stopped her car and tried to befriend them. But they were proud of their high caste and did not want help from a "polluted" one.

One day, to her delight, a large group of men approached her car when she stopped. But alas, they were bringing her a sick bullock. She was filled with consternation that they would bring her the bullock, but not their ill children. But she would not fail them, for she knew a bullock was extremely important to them.

Grimly she said, "I'll do what I can." But the bullock kicked and glared in a frightening fashion each time she approached it.

Finally, the men threw the bullock to the ground and sat on it! Dr. Ida took out her instruments and carefully removed an ugly tumor from the beast's ear. She fervently prayed for the operation to be a success.

The next week when she returned to Lathery, a crowd was waiting for her—a crowd of people!

The needs were vast, and the people ignorant, but Ida kept on faithfully doing what she could, and she trained many others to help her in the work.

(to be continued)

Why did the first little boy come to Dr. Ida?

Why did Dr. Ida take time to help a bullock?

It may look glamorous to be a missionary, but mission work is hard. Today, are you remembering to faithfully do the work that is your duty to do?

Jesus went about doing good. What are you doing?

Read Romans 12:10, 11.

Galatians 6:10: "As we have therefore opportunity, let us do good to all men, especially unto them who are of the household of faith."

Save That Baby!

Ida's mother, Sophia Scudder, was sorting pills on the veranda and looked up in surprise when Ida came home with a baby girl in her arms.

"I just rescued this baby in the hospital," Ida said. "I had a strong impression that I should go and check on this baby, who had been ill but was now ready to go home.

"The grandmother and mother were trying to smother their child. I yelled, 'No, No!' They loosened their grip, but when I reached for the baby, she was already turning blue!

"Mother," Ida wailed, "I was horrified! I had worked so hard to save this baby when she was sickly at birth. I asked them how they could deliberately destroy such a precious, innocent baby?

"The grandmother defiantly spat on the ground and muttered, 'She is better off dead. A child born on an unlucky day is meant to die; it is the will of Allah.' A shrewd look crossed her face. 'If you don't want this child to die, take her, she is yours, but bad luck will follow her.'

"I looked to the mother, and she consented. 'Take the baby from me, please,' she said. 'Hopefully my next baby will be favored by Allah and be born on a holy day.'

"I told them that any day a baby is born is a holy day, and I also said I would take the baby if they wished to give her away. So that is the explanation, mother, for why this child is in my arms. But now, what am I to do with this baby?"

Unusual situations were no surprise to Sophia, who had been a missionary in India for many, many years. "Just do what any mother does with a baby. Feed her, give her a name. Take one step at a time. Things will work out," Sophia wisely counseled.

Ida named the little girl Mary, and she soon grew to be a smiling, chubby child. Before long, she was joined by three more little girls who also were given to Ida.

Dr. Ida Scudder had not meant to start an orphanage, but she could not turn away an innocent little one who was doomed to death or corruption.

"I cannot refuse these children," Ida said. "If I refuse them, they would be sold to temples to be brought up in the midst of terrible sin and evil. Jesus took time for children. He held the little ones in his arms and blessed them. I am endeavoring to follow in the footsteps of my Master."

read and consider...

What would have happened if Ida had not listened to God prompting her to check on the baby?
Why did Ida care about the babies?
What work are you called to do for Jesus?

Read Isaiah 40:11, and Psalm 127.
Luke 16:10: "He that is faithful in that which is least, is faithful also in much."

Bell's Diet

The habits that are formed and the decisions that are made in one's youth profoundly impact the rest of one's life.

Isobel was a Canadian girl who felt God's call to be a missionary to China. She was born in Toronto in 1901. Her nickname was *Bell*.

Theresa, Bell's eight-year-old student, was gleefully drinking pop and eating candy and ice cream when Bell met her at the store.

"Oh, my dear," Bell remarked, "you won't be hungry for a good, hot dinner if you fill up on junk food."

"This is much better," laughed the girl, as she kept eating candy and sipping the cold pop.

Later, Bell wondered what was wrong with her life. "Your Word bores me, Lord. You seem to have forsaken me." Suddenly, in her mind, she saw the little girl feeding on junk food. She was smitten with a thought, *Am I like that, feeding my spirit on the junk food of playing cards, attending movies, and reading love stories?*"

One dark night John 6:67, 68 gripped her: "Lord, to whom shall we go? thou hast the words of eternal life."

God spoke to her, "Would you rather have those things or Me?"

"Do you want to completely belong to the world, do as you please, or have me?"

"Do you want the friendship of the world or my companionship?"

"Do you want to drift or be anchored?"

"Do you want to spend life or invest it?"

Bell covered her face with her hands. "Lord," she cried out, "there is no one and nothing I want, but You." From that day on, Bell quit the junk food of worthless books, cards, and movies. She searched God's Word and grew to love it more and more.

read and consider...

Why is it so important for us to know, read, and memorize the Word of God?

Read: Psalm 119: 9–16.

Joshua 1:8: "This book of the law shall not depart out of thy mouth; but thou shalt meditate therein day and night, that thou mayest observe to do according to all that is written therein: for then thou shalt make thy way prosperous, and then thou shalt have good success."

Take time to read worthwhile books about missionaries. For more about Bell, read *Isobel Kuhn* (the Canadian girl who felt God's call to the Lisu people of China) by Lois Hoadley Dick, Bethany House, 1987.

People or Possessions?

John and Isobel Kuhn were young missionaries. Newly married, they were excited about setting up furniture in their first home in China.

Bell, as Isobel was called, greatly enjoyed setting up the new rattan furniture in their room. She draped her beautiful quilt, a gift from a friend, over her trunk. She placed a pretty rug from home on the floor. "I don't mind being a poor missionary," she mused, "but at least I can make this room look attractive."

That same week, Bell heard a knock on her door. Delighted, she invited eight Chinese peasant women into her house. She served them tea. She had studied the Chinese language for one and a half years, and she presented the Gospel story to them the best she could. How happy she was that the women actually understood her words.

But then something happened that took the sunshine out of Bell's day. The oldest of the Chinese women had perched on the trunk. She casually blew her nose into her hand and wiped it off on Bell's beautiful quilt! Bell's stomach churned as she saw the ugly blob of greenish mucus on her prized quilt.

Now she better understood the words the mission director had said to her days before. "Bell, if I had a new quilt, I would throw it away."

Chinese customs were hitting Belle full in the face, for next, a mother held her baby gingerly away from her so that a yellow stream could soak into the rug. Her new rug was stained and ruined, yet the Chinese women had no idea they had offended Bell. She smiled weakly and bowed as the women left.

Beautiful things are lovely, Bell thought, *but if I value things more than people, then my precious possessions must go.*

So Bell sold the rattan furniture and bought plain chairs and benches like her Chinese neighbors used.

She often reminded herself to die daily as she fought lice, bedbugs, and mosquitoes. How she missed indoor plumbing and many other comforts she was accustomed to!

She disciplined her mind by memorizing Scripture verses. The precious promise of Galatians 2:8 helped her change. "For he that wrought effectually in Peter . . . the same was mighty in me."

John and Bell served faithfully in China for many years. They confronted many hardships: war, illness, and long separations. Yet through all these things, their faithful witness led countless Chinese to the Lord they loved.

read and consider...

Why did Bell decide it was best to get rid of her beautiful things? Ponder this thought: It is a kindness that God does not enable us to see the future but gives us strength to trust Him for one day at a time.

Read: Philippians 4:8-10.
Philippians 4:13: "I can do all things through Christ which strengtheneth me."

chapter three

Better Than Gold

They Loved God's Word

What Really Matters

A short man with a beaming smile stood at the entrance of the Calvary Bible School chapel. As the students filed in for morning worship, Brother Ervin Hershberger, the principal, had a cheery greeting and handshake for each one.

Ervin could greet all of the students at Calvary Bible School by name. His memory was exceptionally keen. As a young dairy farmer, he had been able to say the birth dates of all his cows. The Lord convicted him that there were better things to memorize. He got to work memorizing Scriptures, the words that really matter.

Ervin and Barbara had only one daughter, Mildred, but Ervin took a keen interest in others' children. In 1964 he was ordained a deacon in the Mountain View congregation. He knew all the first and middle names of each child in church. He prayed for all the children and members of his church regularly.

He had more time for prayer when he sold his dairy farm in 1967. This freed him from material obligations to do work with eternal value, the work that really matters.

In 1970 he helped establish Calvary Bible School in Arkansas. For the next 26 years, he and Barbara spent from three to four months of every year there. He was a teacher, academic dean, principal, and board member. Barbara supported his calling, though she loved best to be at home. She faithfully gave herself to secretarial work at the school.

He was a man who did things wholeheartedly. At Bible school he would jump rope each day in order to stay physically fit for the service of God. He was a man of prayer, praying for the students by name.

Ervin loved to study and teach the Word of God. He was a lifelong student of the Bible, the Book that really matters. He loved God with all his heart and wanted God to be glorified in all he did.

In his sunset years, he still had a passion to study and teach the Word of God. He wrote four books and taught his series on the Old Testament Tabernacle at many churches. He taught a weekly Bible class at a local nursing home when health and weather permitted.

Ervin had an intense desire to die in the harness rather than in the hospital. His desire was granted September 3, 2003. He was 89 years old, helping with churchhouse cleaning, when God called him home.

read and consider...

Why did Ervin sell his farm?
What was his reason for jumping rope?
What did he do when he was elderly?

Read Matthew 6:33 and John 6:27.
Colossians 3:23: "And whatsoever ye do, do it heartily, as to the
    Lord, and not unto men."

It Ain't Too Hot

Do you fidget and squirm when the minister preaches extra long? When there are numerous testimonies do you impatiently eye the clock and long to get home to your delicious Sunday dinner and free time?

It was a hot, humid summer day. Edwin Troyer and a group of youth were on their way to a ladies' prison in Marysville, Ohio, to conduct a worship service.

The room where the service was held was stifling and sticky warm, and there was no air conditioning. Edwin asked, "Is the heat bothering you today?" Many raised their hands in affirmation. "Well," Edwin responded, "we can cut the service shorter and not sing as many hymns as usual."

A young lady close to the front raised her hand and said, "It ain't too hot."

In that bleak prison existence, she was thirsty for more. She longed for more of the cool refreshing stream of living water that comes from God.

Paul A. Miller once shared this list of PRACTICAL PREP-ARATIONS FOR WORSHIP:
1. Start preparing for worship on Saturday.
2. When possible, be at home Saturday evening.
3. Get adequate rest to be alert Sunday morning.
4. Meditate on the Word and pray.
5. Arrive at church in time to calm your spirit.

6. Listen attentively.

7. Come on the lookout for God.

8. Leave on the lookout for people.

Do we hunger for more, even though we can so freely attend church?

What can make us greatly appreciate the privilege of attending church?

Read Matthew 5:6 and Isaiah 55:6.

Jeremiah 15:16: "Thy words were found, and I did eat them: and thy word was unto me the joy and rejoicing of mine heart: for I am called by thy name, O LORD God of hosts."

His Heavy Load

An elderly deacon came to Master's International Ministries mission in Kiev, Ukraine. He asked for Bibles and Christian literature for his church. This man had been a Christian for 42 years. Bibles had been scarce during the reign of communism.

The mission gave him 24 Bibles. He was overwhelmed with the gift and filled with joy. He was also given 40 copies of the book *101 Favorite Stories from the Bible*.

This man was too poor to call for a taxi to take him back to his village. His great desire to take God's Word to his church made him do what seemed impossible for an old man. He tied together the tops of the two bags containing the 24 Bibles and 40 Bible storybooks. With help, he hung them over his shoulder. Then he staggered away under his heavy load to the bus stop to return to his people.

The Best News

A lady from Romania shared that one morning her husband told her he was convinced that this day they were to receive some good news. Of course she was delighted, for like ladies everywhere, she loved good news.

The news for that dear couple was not "common news." It was a gift, an unspeakable one, a Bible! A much desired and longed for Bible, a real Bible!

"If only you could have seen my husband kissing it and touching that Bible tenderly!" she wrote.

"My husband is over 70 years old now and still goes with the Gospel through the villages and other places, sharing the best news of all."

Christian Aid Ministries newsletter stories, 2000.
Used by permission.

read and consider...

How many Bibles are in your home?
Praise God for the true riches that are yours.

Read: Psalm 63:1–6.
Psalm 119:47, 48: "And I will delight myself in thy command-
    ments, which I have loved. My hands also will I lift up unto
    thy commandments, which I have loved; and I will meditate
    in thy statutes.

His Best Treasure

*What do you think a sixteen-year-old boy would want
more than anything else? What do you treasure most of all?*

Sixteen-year-old Yun lived in Communist China in 1975.
Owning a Bible or talking about Jesus was strictly forbidden.
But when Yun's father became seriously ill, the family cried
out to Jesus for help. His father was miraculously healed.

Yun asked his mother who Jesus really was. She could
not read, and they had no Bible, but she said, "Jesus is the
Son of God. Think of Him. He died on the cross, taking all
our sins and sickness for us. His teachings are written in the
Bible."

"Mother," Yun said, "are there any words of Jesus left? I
want to read them for myself."

Sadly his mother replied, "No, His words are all gone.
For all I know there is nothing left of His teachings."

The Word of God was scarce in those days in Communist China, and even today Bibles are still scarce in China.

Yun's mother and friends did not know what a Bible
looked like. Only a handful of elderly Christians could
remember seeing a Bible years ago. But they did remember
some of God's words passed down by faithful Christian men
and women.

More than anything else, Yun wanted a Bible.

Yun's mother went with him to visit an aged man who
had been a church leader before the Cultural Revolution. It
was a long walk to his home. They told the man, "We want
to see the Word of God. Do you have a Bible?"

The man looked fearful at the request. He had spent 20 years in prison for his faith. Anyone caught with God's Word would be beaten, his family would be beaten, and the Bible burned.

The old pastor told Yun, "If you want a Bible, pray to God in heaven. It is a heavenly book, and only God can give you one. God rewards those who seek Him with all their heart."

Every evening, for more than a month, Yun knelt and prayed, "Lord, please give me a Bible, please give me a Bible." But Yun still had no Bible.

Yun went back to the old pastor. He told him, "I have prayed as you said, and still I have no Bible. Please show me yours. I would be happy and content to at least see the Word of God."

The pastor replied, "Yun, to be serious you must not only pray, but fast and weep to the Lord."

For the next 100 days, Yun prayed for a Bible—crying to God like a hungry child does to his father. He ate only a small bowl of rice every evening. One night he had a vision that some men gave him bread which turned into a Bible when he put in into his mouth.

Early one morning two strangers came to his door. They had a Bible for Yun. God had shown another pastor that he should give his hidden Bible to Yun. It had taken him months to decide to obey what the Lord told him to do with his Bible.

The Bible was most precious to Yun. He devoured it hungrily. He was overjoyed that God heard and answered his prayers. Yun spent much time memorizing Scripture, hiding God's precious Word in his heart. He spoke of God's

Word to his friends and neighbors. His faith had to be shared. But then, one sad day Yun was arrested.

(to be continued)

read and consider...

What is your greatest treasure?
Will it still be important to you when you are old?

Read Psalm 19:7–11.
Psalm 119:9: "Wherewithal shall a young man cleanse his way? by taking heed thereto according to thy word."

A Dark, Dingy Cell

Yun's Bible was taken away, and he was thrown into prison.

Yun spent many long years in prison. But even in prison, he kept his faith and witnessed for Jesus Christ. Miraculously, he survived cruel beatings, lack of food, and horrible living conditions.

One day in prison he prayed, "Oh, Lord, I ask you one thing. Please send me your Word, a Bible, in this dark and dismal cell. Oh, how I long for your Words."

That day, Yun suffered yet again for his faith. God told him to patiently endure because of the Word of God and the testimony of Jesus.

Yun dreamed that his handcuffs fell off, and he was reading a Bible. In his dream, he preached, and gave thanks to God in heaven.

When Yun awoke, he told the Lord he loved him and prayed yet again for a Bible. His handcuffs fell off. That very day, the prison director came to his cell and said, "Yun, we had a meeting yesterday. We decided to give you a Bible. Study it well and repent of your crimes."

Yun knelt, and with tears streaming down his face, he thanked God for this extraordinary answer to prayer. He had never heard of a prisoner who was allowed to have a Bible. Yet, God had sent him one.

He was deeply encouraged to know that God had not forgotten him. He thought back to how God had answered his prayer for a Bible when he was 16 years old.

Now he was 30 years old, alone and lonely in a small, dark and dingy cell. He realized anew that there is no limit to God's provision and power.

Reource: *The Heavenly Man.* Brother Yun with Paul Hattaway, 2002, Monarch Books.

read and consider...

What would happen in our homes if parents and children had an intense desire to read and obey the Word of God?

Why don't we hunger more for God's Word?

What about modern entertainment: T.V., movies, videos, and computer games? Can all the animation and noise dull the senses and make the pure and holy Word of God of little appeal?

Can unhealthy reading material and novels have the same effect?

Read Luke 10:39, 42.

1 Peter 5:7: "Casting all your care upon him, for he careth for you."

Mama Loved God's Word

"What a blessing to think of my Mama in heaven," my friend Fannie shared. "She could hardly wait to see the Lord. It kept her going through life's trials to think that someday she would see Jesus. I can just imagine her singing in the heavenly choir, for my Mama loved to sing!

"Her life had so many hardships and disappointments, but through it all, Mama clung to God. God was the source of her strength. In my mind I see her yet, sitting on the sofa with her Bible. I don't remember Mama reading anything but the Bible! Mama had a passion for the Bible, a deep, intense longing and love for God and His Word.

"Mama took her children to school each morning, then went to her job at the sewing factory. Work was difficult, but she needed to help provide for the family. When Mama came home from work, the children all knew she would go to her bedroom to pray. She could hardly wait for that time with God. She would close the door, fall on her knees and audibly pour out her heart to God."

Fannie remembers standing outside her mother's bedroom, leaning against the door. She loved to listen as her mother prayed and cried to God above. Mama's prayers were a comfort, a rock of strength and security in a home where the father was not emotionally stable. Yet, they were a close-knit family.

Fannie's mama knew the power of prayer. She was a genuine prayer warrior. Fannie's sister Naomi was plagued with an awful, persistent toothache one night. How it ached! She cried and cried in pain, unable to fall asleep. Naomi said, "Mama, let's pray." Rebecca prayed fervently for her daughter and dabbed a little iodine on the tooth. The toothache went away!

Months later, another tooth began to ache. Again they prayed for God to take the ache away. The tooth continued to ache. The next day Rebecca said, "We are going to the dentist." This was a most unusual decision, for they could not afford it.

The kind dentist examined Naomi, then he said, "Who put that filling in the other tooth?"

"We have never been to the dentist before," Rebecca stated.

"It must have been the man upstairs," the dentist replied.

"Yes," Rebecca affirmed. "If there is a filling in that tooth, the Lord must have put it there!"

Many years later, Fannie said she believes God prompted her mom to go to the dentist so that God's power could be shown. It was an incident of encouragement, a real strengthening to their faith.

Mama loved to tell others that story as a testimony to the goodness of God. God cares, even when a tooth aches.

(to be continued)

read and consider...

What does it mean to have a passion for God's Word?
What wonderful things do Rebecca's children remember about her?

Read Psalm 18:1–6.
Proverbs 18:10: "The name of the Lord is a strong tower: the righteous runneth into it, and is safe."
Proverbs 14:26: "In the fear of the Lord is strong confidence: and his children shall have a place of refuge."

Mama Loved to Witness

Fannie's mama Rebecca loved to witness to anyone with whom she came in contact. She shared with others how God touched and filled her daughter's tooth. She took gospel tracts and literature along to the sewing factory and testified to the other women who worked there. She and another lady got together at lunch break to sing and pray.

Rebecca came from a family of 14 children. In later years, when she and her sisters got together, they often spent time in prayer. It was beautiful. Rebecca's sister Fannie also had a deep love for the Word of God. She would sit down to read and pray for an hour. She would be so blessed and enjoying the Word that it was hard to quit and begin the day's duties.

A niece once asked her, "How do you get to loving God's Word like you do?" Fannie replied, "Pray, sincerely pray, that God would give you a hunger and thirst for Him and His Word."

Rebecca loved to sing praises to God. She could hardly sing without raising her hands in adoration to her Father. Her children often heard their mother singing. She was also a dedicated Sunday school teacher.

I recall the times she was at tent meetings in our area. When the congregation stood to sing, she joined right in and, without embarrassment, she raised her hands. Her sole focus was on worshiping God.

Another unusual incident that touched and blessed Rebecca's family occurred while they were living in Maryland. One Sunday morning, Rebecca's seven-year-old, Mary Ann, could not walk. Her father carried her to church, and Mary Ann felt ashamed and helpless. Why couldn't she walk?

Uncle Dan (a minister) and his wife were in church that day. After the services, Rebecca's husband Amos asked his brother if he would pray for Mary Ann. They took the little girl to a prayer room. Dan laid his hands on her and fervently implored the Lord to heal Mary Ann. God heard and answered their prayers.

When Mary Ann was an adult, she worked at a nursing home. One day she was assisting a lady who could not walk. Caringly, Mary Ann asked her if she had not been able to walk from birth. The lady told her she had been stricken with polio. Mary Ann wondered if polio was the reason she could not walk those long years ago. Had God spared her from the ravages of that dreaded disease?

Many years later, at a reunion, Mary Ann asked her Uncle Dan if he remembered how he prayed for her years ago. Tears rolled down his cheeks and he responded, "God touched you!"

read and consider...

Are you singing and sharing with others because you love the Lord?

Can others tell that you love Jesus?

Read Psalm 107:1, 2.

James 5:15, 16: "And the prayer of faith shall save the sick, and the Lord shall raise him up; and if he have committed sins, they shall be forgiven him. Confess your faults one to another, and pray one for another, that ye may be healed. The effectual fervent prayer of a righteous man availeth much."

The Wheel That Didn't Fit

Two brothers, Alex and Anton, were driving through the Ukrainian city of Kiev with precious cargo. There were Bibles hidden in their car! They were taking the Bibles to their sister's house. The Bibles could not remain long in one place lest they be discovered. Others would come and get them and share them with people who were longing for the Word of God.

Just as Alex and Anton entered the heart of Kiev, one of the car's wheels fell off and rolled some distance away. They jolted to a stop and retrieved the wheel, all the while wondering why this had happened. They prayed, again asking God for His protection, and then they set to work putting the wheel back on. The wheel just would not fit. They sweated and pushed for a long time, trying to get it back on. They could not understand what was wrong. The wheel had been on the car, now surely they could get it back into place! Suddenly, it just slipped on. They tightened the lugs and were on their way.

It was 12:30 when they finally pulled up to their sister's house. They were hours behind schedule for the Bible delivery. Alona met them at the door. She was crying and thanking God that they were late. She told them that the KGB, the state police, had been tipped off that Bibles were to be at her house. The police had come and were waiting for the Bibles and the men who brought them!

"Oh, my brothers," Alona cried, "the KGB left just 30 minutes ago. They waited here for hours. Finally, they got tired and left. I praise God that you were late!"

Anton and Alex looked at each other. "That is why we couldn't get that wheel back on!" they exclaimed. "God was protecting His Bibles, our sister, and us! We could not understand it, but God knew how to detain us!"

Inside the house they fell on their knees and thanked God for His protection. They praised Him for the promise in Romans 8:28: "And we know that all things work together for good to them that love God, to them who are the called according to His purpose."

Resource: *Master's International Ministries newsletter,* May, 2005.

Resource: *Master's International Ministries newsletter,* May, 2005.

read and consider...

Is the Word of God very precious to you?
Why were the brothers willing to take a great risk to deliver Bibles?

Read: Matthew 6:33, 34 and Psalm 19:7–10.
Matthew 24:35: "Heaven and earth shall pass away, but my words shall not pass away."

From Soles to Souls

A long, long time ago, in the 1700's, there was a cobbler living in England who made and mended shoes. He was different from most cobblers, for while he was mending folks' old shoes, his thoughts went traveling all around the world.

On the wall beside his workbench was a map he had made from brown wrapping paper. He often would look at the map and think about the people who lived in strange lands far from England. He drew small pictures on the map and pasted little clippings of information he found about different people groups.

Even when this cobbler, William Carey, was a little boy, he delighted in hearing stories about people in faraway lands. His friends loved to hear him repeat these stories to them.

Another unusual thing about his cobbler shop was the open Bible Carey kept beside him on his bench. As he worked and glanced at his map, he thought about the people in lands so far away. Then William's eyes were drawn to his Bible. The words, "Go ye into all the world, and preach the gospel to every creature," seemed to leap out at him, sounding again and again in his ears.

"Some preacher must go and tell the savages about Jesus," he thought.

He was a cobbler, not a preacher. He did not think of going himself, but God was preparing him.

After thinking so much about the heathen and Christ's command, "Go ye," Carey mustered enough courage to attend a gathering of many preachers. He told them how the two little words "go ye" kept repeating in his mind, and how he felt that someone should go. But in all that large crowd, no one seemed to feel as he did.

Sadly he returned to his cobbler bench. But he could not forget the two little words, "Go ye." He could not forget the people in far-away lands who had never heard of Jesus.

One day the poor cobbler felt led to preach a sermon at a large meeting. His title was, "Expect Great Things From God." His sermon spoke to the hearts of the people; finally they were led to obey Jesus' command, "go ye." They raised enough money to send a missionary to India, and the man they chose to send was none other than William Carey.

It took Carey five months to reach India in 1793. When he arrived, there was no one to welcome him, not one person who seemed glad that he had come! The sights, the sounds, and the language were all very strange and new. Yet he could see and feel more deeply than ever how the people needed to know about Jesus.

First of all, William had to learn the language of India. He went to a village school where little brown boys sat in the warm sand and wrote the letters of the Hindi alphabet on the ground with their fingers. He ran out of money and worked in a factory. He preached to hundreds of Indian men with whom he worked. He walked to 200 villages and preached the gospel.

Every chance he had, he worked on a dictionary and a translation of the Bible, so that many more people could learn the good news from heaven.

For seven long years, not one person to whom he preached was willing to give up his old ways and come to Jesus. Discouragement did not stop him. Carey kept right on showing the love of God and sharing his message. Slowly, slowly the light began to dawn in the hearts of the Indians. More and more people began to understand the love of God and why Carey was willing to leave his home and friends to tell them about Jesus.

For 40 years, William Carey faithfully worked and preached in India.

Resource: *Words of Cheer,* Herald Press, Scottdale, Pennsylvania, July, 1944.

read and consider...

Who should go tell the lost about Jesus today?
Who didn't Carey give up when no one became a Christian for seven years?
Will you be willing to serve Jesus WHEREVER He leads you?

Read Matthew 28:19, 20 and Acts 1:8.
Matthew 9:38: "Pray ye therefore the Lord of the harvest, that he will send forth labourers into his harvest."

The Preacher Without a Bible

Wouldn't you be surprised if your preacher walked to the front of your church next Sunday without a Bible? If your church had an ordination, would a man be chosen who could not read? God moves in mysterious ways to perform His work in the world!

If you were to visit a church in Nakuru, Kenya, you would likely see a tall black man walk up front to preach, and his hands would be empty. Empty? Well, why carry a Bible if you cannot read? This preacher, Joseph Musikali, cannot read! But he has what is most important, a heart full of love for God, and a heart that has God's Word hidden in it!

The wonderful and amazing thing is that Joseph knows his Bible better than most of us who can read! His sense of memory is so keen that he knows many, many Scriptures and their references by heart.

Every day, Joseph's daughter reads to him from God's Holy Book. He files those Scriptures away in his memory. If a church brother needs to know where a certain verse is found, he can just ask Joseph where to find it.

Joseph is a man of unfeigned faith. Genuine faith. Simple faith. What a challenge and a blessing to see how God has called this man to preach the wonderful words of life!

read and consider...

Are you taking time to memorize Scripture?
Why is it good to hide God's Word in your heart?

Read: Psalm 119:97–104.
Psalm 1:2: "His delight is in the law of the Lord, and in his law doth he meditate day and night."

Starved for the Word

China has vast multitudes of people. Bibles are scarce. If we could send two million Bibles a year to China, it would take over ten years to provide every believer with a Bible. Even though there is a severe shortage of Bibles, many people in China are coming to the glorious light of God.

Here are two little stories of Chinese people who lacked Bible and how they loved God's Word and longed for Bible of their own.

Christmas Eve Gift

On Christmas Eve, 2001, 3,000 copies of *101 Favorite Stories from the Bible* were distributed to children in China. A man came and asked, "May I also have one? I don't have a child, neither do I have a Bible." The longing for a Bible was written on his face. He was given one of the Bible storybooks.

He opened the book, and his tears began to flow. "How long I have been waiting to read about Jesus—how long!" Right then and there, he sat down and started reading. He read through the night, on and on, until he had finished all 101 stories around daybreak on Christmas Day.

Praying for Years

"My dear people," Pastor Chun said, "we do not understand why it is so difficult for us to get more Bibles. We have prayed for many years. Let us continue to pray."

One glad day, 40 boxes of Bibles were sent to that country church in which 90 percent of the people did not even own a New Testament.

Pastor Chun was weeping and laughing and thanking God for His goodness. As the people received Bibles, their very own Bibles, their faces beamed with excitement, like little children at Christmas time. Tears ran down their faces as they reverently clasped their own copies of God's Holy Word, for Chinese Christians are starved for the Word of God.

Christian Aid Ministries newsletter stories.
Used by permission.

read and consider...

Is the Bible precious to us in America?
Why do we need to read God's Word?
Pray for the people who deliver Bibles to China.

Read: Matthew 5:6 and 2 Timothy 2:15.
Psalm 119:47: "I will delight myself in thy commandments,
    which I have loved."

Nature Shouts His Praise

But ask now the beasts, and they shall teach thee;
and the fowls of the air, and they shall tell thee:
Or speak to the earth, and it shall teach thee:
and the fishes of the sea shall declare unto thee.
Who knoweth not in all these that the
hand of the Lord hath wrought this?
In whose hand is the soul of every living thing,
and the breath of all mankind.

Job 12:7–10

He Loved Snow

His father and his brother just could not understand Willie's fascination with snow! They were dairy farmers in Vermont in the late 1800's. They thought it would be much more profitable for Willie to keep at his work!

Willie liked to study the clouds and the temperatures. When he knew a snow storm was coming, he rejoiced, for he loved snow most of all! The thought of snow made him warm to the tips of his toes.

For over 50 years, Wilson A. Bentley loved to study the marvels of our Creator's little snowflakes. He was a short, quiet man. His heart was full of love for God and the wonders of creation, especially snow!

As a boy, Willie was fascinated with studying birds, trees, and the weather. He collected rocks and minerals whenever he had spare time from farm chores. But most of all, he loved to study snow!

Jericho, Vermont, where Willie lived, is one of the snowiest places on earth! The area receives an average of 120 inches of snow each year! This boy who loved snow was born in God's greatest snow laboratory.

Willie was 15 years old when his mother gave him a microscope. What fun it was to study flowers, drops of dew, a bee's wing, and water from the brook. But what he really wanted to see with his microscope was, you guessed it, snow!

At the first snowfall, Willie was ready. Gently he scooped up a wee snowflake and slid it under the lens. What he saw that day took his breath away! Such intricate beauty he had not imagined. He was excited and overwhelmed! Each tiny flake was a work of art by the master artist. No two were identical. Each had a new shape and pattern, though each had six identical sides. Over the years, Willie found snowflakes with designs more delicate than lace. Some had fruit, birds or other animals in their design. Willie felt he must find a way to share with the world the beauty of snowflakes. For three winters he did his best to carefully draw them, laboring away in a cold shed, for the snowflakes melted so quickly, and then the beautiful design was gone. Finally, he had 300 drawings. They were good, yet he felt they were not good enough.

Leafing through a catalog one day, Willie saw a microscope that was also a camera. He caught his breath. This was just the thing he needed to help him document the true beauty of snow. His parents scrimped and saved to purchase that microscope for his 17th birthday. It cost one hundred dollars, a large sum in those days. Willie was thrilled!

After much practice and experimenting, Willie finally learned how to take clear pictures of snow. Over time, Willie became an expert on snow, taking over 400 photomicrographs of snowflakes! No one else had ever taken a single photograph of a snowflake!

When Willie turned 66 years old in 1931, one of his greatest dreams came true. His book entitled *Snow Crystals* was published. It contained 2,500 of his best snowflake photos. He calmly said, "Now the world can glorify God for the treasures of the snow." His goal of revealing to the world the mystery and grandeur of the snowflake was accomplished.

Resource: *Snow Never Milked a Cow* by Dalan E. Decker in Young Companion, January, 2006.

Take time to enjoy the beauties of a snowflake.

Isn't it lovely how the fresh, pure whiteness of a snowfall brightens the drab winter landscape?

Read: Job 37:5, 6 and Isaiah 1:18.

Job 38:22: "Hast thou entered into the treasures of the snow? or
hast thou seen the treasures of the hail?"

We Must Have It

All mankind must have water. Without water there would be no life. A man can live without food for more than two months, but he can live without water for only about seven days.

Drinking ten glasses of water daily helps to keep you in good health. An average person takes in about 16,000 gallons of water in his lifetime.

Water covers more than 70% of the earth's surface. It fills the oceans, rivers, and lakes. It is in the ground and in the air we breathe.

Again, without water, there would be no life. Your body is 65% water. Food contains much water: a chicken is 75% water, a pineapple is about 80% water, and a tomato is 95% water.

Throughout history, water has been people's slave and master. Civilizations rise when water is plentiful. They fall when the supply fails. People have fought over water. Sadly, some have worshiped rain gods and implored false gods to send rain.

When rains fail, crops wither and starvation may stalk the land. On the other hand, when it rains too heavily, flooding can cause much death and loss.

Industries consume huge amounts of water. It takes about 80 gallons of water to make one Sunday newspaper and approximately 20 gallons to produce one pound of steel.

The United States has more homes with running water than any other country in the world. For many people in

Asia and in South and Central America, indoor running water would be a great luxury. They must get their water from the village well or carry it from pools or rivers far from home.

In mountainous villages in Haiti, many homes are one hour or more from their water source. People trudge up steep trails carrying on their heads all the water they use each day. What a daily chore! The goats and cows are led out once a day for water. On hot days, the animals could easily drink more water, but they must wait for their once-a-day drink. To Haitians, water is very precious indeed. It is never wasted.

Yes, water is vital and life-giving. We must have it! Thank God for your daily supply of water.

read and consider...

Be very grateful for the abundance of water in your home. Have you tasted the best water, the living waters of God?

Read Psalm 42:1, 2 and John 4:13, 14.
Psalm 63:1: "Oh God, thou art my God; early will I seek thee: my soul thirsteth for thee in a dry and thirsty land where no water is."

Ants for Lunch

Imagine having a sticky tongue two feet long to help you scoop up the food you like the best. Imagine having such sharp hearing that you can detect the footfalls of a thousand marching termites. Imagine having a sense of smell 40 times stronger than your current sense of smell. (You could easily find the chocolates your mom has hidden!) Imagine your favorite meal to be 30,000 ants or termites a day!

God created an amazing creature called the aardvark, the giant anteater of South Africa. The aardvark can hear and smell exceptionally well. Its tongue is long and sticky which makes it possible for it to capture its favorite meal of ants and termites.

The aardvark is a strange looking animal. It has long ears like a donkey's and a snout like a hog's. Its body is four to six feet long. A thin coat of hair covers its thick skin. You could not pick it up and carry it around, for it weighs around 140 pounds. Its legs are short and its claws strong.

The aardvark's mighty claws are a most handy tool. When an aardvark needs a fast food meal, it rips open nests of ants and termites with its claws. Its long, sticky tongue sneaks down into the nest and snares those squirming ants and termites.

The aardvark lives in a hole in the ground. It is a fast digger. It can dig a hole much faster than most animals can. In a few minutes, it can burrow deep enough to escape from its enemies, for lions enjoy a meal of tasty aardvark. Some people like to eat them too.

The aardvark is not a fierce animal. But do not try to start a fight, for it can roll on its back and use its powerful claws to defend itself.

read and consider...

The aardvark does exactly what God created it to do.
What about you? Do you do each day what you know God
  wants you to?
If you don't know what God wants you to do, try discussing His
  will for you with your parents.

Read Ephesians 6:1–3.
Ephesians 5:1, 2: "Be ye therefore followers of God, as dear
  children; and walk in love, as Christ also hath loved us."

No Teeth At All

Have you ever heard of a pangolin? It is similar in many ways to the aardvark. The pangolin loves to eat ants and is found in Asia, Africa, and Indonesia. Like the aardvark, the pangolin has large, strong claws on its forefeet, just perfect to rip open the nests of ants and termites.

Pangolins, like other anteaters, have no teeth at all. Instead of teeth, tough plates in their stomachs grind the insects. Their stomachs churn and squeeze. You would think they would have a bellyache!

A pangolin has very unique looks. His body is covered with hard plates (or horny scales) like an armadillo that provide protection. If an enemy attacks, the pangolin rolls into a tight ball. It is so heavily armored that most times it is unharmed.

The pangolin's snout is long and narrow and its tail is long, varying in length from three to five feet. His rope-like tongue is long and sticky, just right to thrust far out to catch those ants the pangolin loves to feast on.

How about pangolin meat for dinner tonight? Many people hunt them for their excellent meat. Thankfully, they are shy and look for food only at night. Otherwise, they might be extinct today.

Anteaters are becoming scarce as human settlers push into their ranges in the grassy plains and damp tropical rain forests of Central and South America.

Will you ever see an anteater? You may see one in the zoo someday or, if you visit Belize, maybe you will see one there, as I did!

Does someone collect ants and termites for zookeep-ers to feed anteaters in the zoo? Would you like such a job? Amazingly, anteaters in the zoo are fed milk, eggs, and meat!

read and consider...

On which day did God create anteaters?
If you need a clue, check Genesis 1:24–31.

Read: Psalm 8.
Psalm 104:24: "O Lord, how manifold are thy works! In wisdom hast thou made them all: the earth is full of thy riches."

Learn From the Lovebird

Just look at that small, colorful parrot! See its bright green and yellow feathers? It is a lovebird. These parrots make good cage pets, but I think they are the happiest in their native home in southern Africa and Madagascar.

Can you guess why they are called lovebirds? Well, when the lovebird takes a mate, they stay together for life. It is very loving to its mate. They show affection by caressing and preening each other with their bills. In fact, the lovebird can always be found with its mate. When one flies off to hunt for fruit or seeds, the other follows. At night they roost together. They are a closely knit pair.

Lovebirds have a unique way of carrying grass or straw back to their love nests. They tuck the straw under their tail feathers, then fly back to their nests with the grass or straw streaming along behind.

Wouldn't it be nice if all married people loved each other so much that they wanted to stay together for life? When rough times came, they would hold fast to their vows in obedience to the Word of God.

God says in His Holy Word that a husband and wife should love and cleave to each other, forsaking all others till death parts them. The man should vow to have only one wife for all his life. The woman should be his helper and companion as long as they both live.

Following God's laws is the best way to live. His way is for our good and blessing.

Thank God if you have parents who love each other. Decide to follow God's laws now and when you are grown.

read and consider...

What is something you like about the lovebird?
What is a law of God you should obey now?
What makes a happy home?

Read: Mark 10:6–9 and Ephesians 5:25.
Genesis 2:24: "Therefore shall a man leave his father and his mother, and shall cleave unto his wife; and they shall be one flesh. "

Five Tricky Questions

Have you ever gone outside on a dark, clear night, looked up into the heavens, and counted the stars? How many are there?

One cold night we went out on our deck and saw many falling stars—that was fascinating and beautiful!

When David was a shepherd boy, he must have enjoyed watching the starry heavens. David wrote about the stars many times in the Psalms.

In Psalm 8:3, 4 he said, "When I consider thy heavens, the work of thy fingers, . . . what is man that thou art mindful of him?"

Now, let's learn more about the stars, the work of God's fingers!

1. How many stars are there?

On a clear night you can see around 3,000 stars. Six thousand stars can be seen from earth without a telescope. We can see only the brightest stars; there are so many more! Using a telescope with a three-inch lens, you can see 600,000 stars. Can you read this number? 200,0 00,000,000,000,000,000? That is 200 billion billion!! Astronomers (people who study stars) with the Hubble telescope can detect billions of stars and more than I billion galaxies. They say there are likely more than 200 billion billion stars.

"He telleth the number of the stars; he calleth them all by their names" (Psalm 147:4). God knows how many stars there are! He even has a name for each one. That is awesome, amazing, astounding! What a mighty God we serve!

2. Who made the twinkling stars?

It may be easy for you to say, "God did!" Of course. Genesis 1:16 says God made two great lights . . . He made the stars also.

It is sad that many people will not acknowledge that God made the stars. My friend took her children to Stark Wilderness Center one Friday evening for a presentation about stars. A man shared a lot of good information.

A little girl piped up with the question, "Who made the stars?"

The man responded, "Now that is a tricky question." He talked about various beliefs, including the big bang. But he would not admit that God made the stars.

Imagine that you made some delicious chocolate chip cookies. Then some friends came to your house and you shared your fresh cookies with them.

If they ask you, "Who made these cookies?" would you say, "That's a tricky question. We can't really say." Or would you say, "There was a big bang, and suddenly these cookies were on our table!"?

Let's praise God for His marvelous creation and the wonders of the starry skies.

3. How big are the stars?

Some small stars are only 10 miles in diameter. Large stars look like tiny stars because they are so far away.

Actually, many stars are enormous! There are stars large enough to fill the gap between earth and sun. That gap is 93 million miles! Some are 865,000,000 miles in diameter.

The sun is a star, the closest star to the earth. It is huge, yet it is only a medium-sized star. Its diameter is about 109 times that of the earth.

The next closest star to earth (Proxima Centauri) is more than 25 million million miles away. A fast jet would take over a million years to fly that far. These distances are so great, I cannot fathom them!

Job said, "Is not God in the height of heaven? And behold the height of the stars, how high they are" (Job 22:12). David said, "The heavens declare the glory of God, and the firmament showeth his handiwork" (Psalm 19:1).

4. Why did God make stars?

He made them to show us His glory and greatness. He provided a star to lead the wise men to the Christ child over 2,000 years ago! Genesis 1 says that stars are for signs and seasons, for days and years. The sun is a star; without its heat, we would freeze. We rejoice in the warmth of its rays.

Can you think of more reasons God created stars?

5. Do stars sing?

Now maybe that is the most tricky star question!

David said, "Praise ye him, sun and moon, praise him all ye stars of light" (Psalm 148:3).

In Job 38:4 and 7, we read that God asked Job, "Where wast thou when I laid the foundations of the earth? declare if thou hast understanding."

Imagine a chorus of 20 billion billion stars singing the praises of their Creator! God wants us to praise Him! He is pleased when we admire the beauties and wonders of His creation and worship Him as Lord of all!

If people don't praise God, He will make even the stars and the stones to sing!

With David we can say, "Oh Lord, our Lord, how excellent is thy name in all the earth!" (Psalm 8:1)

Can we see all the stars at one time?

How do we know God made the stars?

Read: Psalm 148.

Psalm 147:4: "He telleth the number of the stars; he calleth them all by their names."

Big Bird, Tiny Bird

The great variety in nature is a source of delight and wonder. Our awesome God, who cares for all mankind, sees even the sparrow fall. The wonders of nature all shout out the greatness of God.

The hummingbirds are the smallest birds in the world. They vary in length from two and one fourth inches to eight and one fourth inches.

Compare the hummingbird to the ostrich, the largest living bird. Ostriches may weigh as much as 345 pounds and grow up to eight feet tall!

Hummingbirds can fly up to 60 mph, hover like a helicopter, fly backwards, forward, and even up and down—at lightning speed. Their wings move up to 70 times a second.

The heavy ostrich cannot fly, but it can run fast—up to 40 mph.

The female hummingbird builds a tiny, delicate, cup-shaped nest, an inch deep and an inch in diameter. She lines her nest with plant down, fur, or feathers. Two little pea-sized eggs are found in the hummingbird's nest. In two weeks, blind and featherless birds hatch. Their parents feed them by putting their slender bills down their throats and regurgitating food.

Vastly different is the ostrich's nest. The male ostrich digs a shallow nest in the ground for his lady ostrich. She lays up to ten big eggs, six inches around and weighing three pounds apiece. The male sits on the eggs at night, while the hen takes her turn during the day.

The ostrich eggs take five or six weeks to hatch. When the chicks are only a month old, they can run as fast as their parents. They join them in eating plants. But if a lizard or a turtle comes too close, they may be gobbled up!

If we could set an ostrich and a hummingbird side-by-side, they would be quite a sight to behold!

Many people love to watch and study the birds. Oh, that it would lead them to praise and worship God, the giver of all good gifts!

read and consider...

How can God care for each person and also see each and
every bird?
Birds' songs praise God. What about your songs?

Read Matthew 10:29–31.
Matthew 6:26: "Behold the fowls of the air: for they sow not, neither do they reap, nor gather into barns; yet your heavenly Father feedeth them. Are ye not much better than they?"

The Ugliest Hog

Which animal would never win a beauty contest, and whose name sounds as strange as it looks? The wart hog!

The wart hog lives in the grasslands of Africa. It has a huge, flat head. Its large, curved tusks (they may be two feet long) warn you not to tangle with the wart hog! Big warts stick out from both sides of the wart hog's head. Its unique coat of pale gray is thinly sprinkled with stiff, brownish-gray hairs. A thin mane of long bristly hair hangs over its back and sides. A large wart hog boar may weigh over 200 pounds and measure 30 inches high at the shoulder.

The wart hog's neck is so short that he must kneel down to eat! He eats roots, plants, bird's eggs, and even small animals.

The wart hog's house is a burrow made by other animals. Often, he must enlarge the burrow before he moves in.

When I taught school in Belize years ago, I learned of another wild pig called a peccary, or musk hog. Peccaries are shy and flee from danger. But if the peccary is cornered, beware! They can fight viciously with their sharp teeth!

The peccary's most unusual feature is a large gland on its arched back, about 8 inches in front of its tail. When they are excited, this gland gives off a small amount of musk. This musk has a strong, very unpleasant odor. At the Belize Zoo, I saw, and smelled, a pen full of peccaries. The odor was so potent that I got away from there fast!

God's interesting and curious creatures are scattered all over the world. We cannot fathom or comprehend the greatness of our Creator. There is so much for us to learn!

read and consider...

Can you think of any other creatures whose names tell about them?
Find the wart hog and peccary in an encyclopedia.

Read: Psalm 8.
Psalm 104:24: "O LORD, how manifold are thy works! In wisdom hast thou made them all: the earth is full of thy riches!"

5

chapter five

The Golden Gates

"Let not your heart be troubled: ye believe in God,
believe also in me.
In my Father's house are many mansions:
if it were not so, I would have told you.
I go to prepare a place for you.
And if I go and prepare a place for you,
I will come again, and receive you unto myself;
that where I am, there ye may be also."
(John 14:1-3)

Missing, One Special Little Lad

Darlene cried when she learned that her dear little baby would be born with Down's syndrome. But the first time she held him, she felt an overwhelming love for him, a love that continued to grow! She could not have fathomed the joy and sunshine he would bring to her home! Accepting his disability at first was difficult, but in four short years, accepting his death was much more difficult. Only a mother who has lost a child in death can really understand this valley of sorrow.

Darlene told me, "It has been nine months since Caleb was called to his heavenly home. Life goes on, even though one special little person is missing. I never dreamed that one little boy could leave such an enormous hole in our home and in our hearts. Caleb was a cheerful little sunbeam, tenderhearted and lovable. He was eager to please. We try to remember that he has only moved to our eternal home. What a joyful reunion we shall have some sweet day!"

March 15, 2005, started out as an ordinary day for Darlene and her little boys. Micah (5) and Caleb (3) were playing happily. Around noon, Micah went outside. Of course, Caleb wanted to go out too.

Darlene bundled him up. As he went out, he said, "Bye, Mom," three times, looking back at her with his excited, happy grin. His big brother was working on a tractor behind the house and said he would watch Caleb.

Soon, Micah wanted to go back into the house. Ronald saw Micah go through the doorway with Caleb right beside him. Ronald thought both boys had gone in.

But Caleb had actually run around the house. He must have made a beeline for the pond and the fishing pole lying on the dock. Darlene reminisced, "I can just imagine his delighted grin as he got ready to fish. We think he must have toppled into the pond on his first attempt to cast out the line. The water was only three feet deep."

Ten minutes after Micah came in, Ronald came in for lunch. Where was Caleb? Darlene thought he was in the house, but they could not find him. A frantic search began. Twenty minutes later, Ronald found him face down in the water. They tried CPR, but their efforts were to no avail.

His mother shared, "We believe that Caleb's dear little spirit went straight up to those golden gates in heaven. Jesus was waiting for him with open arms of love. How precious! No more struggles or frustrations on this old earth."

Though the parting is painful and heart rending, though we shed many tears, we are sure that every minute of that Tuesday was allowed by God. We accept it without question. Heaven is nearer than ever before. We realize anew that each one of our children is a gift from God—a gift He calls home in His own good time.

(to be continued)

read and consider...

When do we need to trust God?

Read: Revelation 21:4 and Isaiah 61:2, 3.

Isaiah 25:8: "He will swallow up death in victory; and the Lord God will wipe away tears from off all faces; and the rebuke of His people will He take away from off all the earth; for the Lord hath spoken it."

Lessons From Caleb

Be Accepting

Caleb's life taught us that children with Down's syndrome are much like other children. They have the same emotions as any other child. Caleb taught us not to focus on a person's disability. Focus on the person. We loved and accepted Caleb, even though he was defective.

We learned to love and accept other Down's syndrome children too. Just like us, they need friends.

Our goal is to learn to see the good in everyone and not to judge others by their abilities or lack of them. Remember, everyone is loved by God. Everyone has a never dying soul.

Be Friendly

Caleb loved going to church. After the service this short little lad would go from bench to bench shaking hands with person after person. Each Sunday, about halfway down the aisle he would meet the preacher, give him a big, warm smile, and shake his hand.

Visitors at church? No problem for Caleb; he would shake their hands and nod his head. It looked like he was bowing to each one.

Respond to Discipline

Caleb was at times stubborn and didn't want to eat his healthy food at mealtime. He would stick out his lower lip and pout. His daddy would discipline him. Caleb was always very sorry and would lay his head on his daddy's shoulder.

One day Caleb decided to go for a walk down their busy road, pushing a little carriage before him. He didn't ask his mama, and she did not realize he was gone until a kind lady drove slowly in the lane with a guilty boy in her car. After the lady left, Caleb received a sound spanking. He needed discipline just like any other child does.

Full of Love

Anyone need a hug? Caleb loved to give warm hugs. One day at church, another little boy pushed Caleb down. One of the ministers said he saw Caleb pick himself up off the floor, walk over to the boy, and give him a hug, not a push or a slap.

"Lord, help me learn that when someone is rude I should give love and kindness in return!"

Love Without Partiality

Caleb had a trusting nature. He loved everyone. No doubt his love tank was full from a family who so dearly loved him. It didn't matter to Caleb what a person looked like. One of his speech therapy teachers had black, frizzy hair and long, red fingernails. Caleb went right over and hugged her. He taught us that if people don't look like you think they should, show them love. They may be black, white, fat or thin. Show love.

Give a Smile

Smile at the world and the world will smile back at you. Caleb was that type of smiling lad. Each morning he woke up with a smile. That was his special way. If Caleb saw someone who was sad or crying, he gave them a hug. His sister said that when she was depressed or discouraged, Caleb brought her smile back by giving her a hug, a kiss, or by teasing her.

Enjoy Your Family

Take time for your siblings. You never know when their last minute might come. Laugh often, make memories. Take your little brother or sister to town with you. Play with them and enjoy them. How precious when parents tell their children good-by and take time for hugs and kisses. No one will ever regret that.

Caleb's six-year-old brother Micah dreamed that Caleb came back to the earth! When he woke up, Caleb was not there. Micah was surprised and sad. He misses his little brother.

What Can You Do?

When you have an opportunity, reach out and be friendly to a Down's syndrome child. You may feel afraid because their mouth turns down at the corners or their eyes are shaped like almonds. They may have small feet and short fingers. Don't be afraid, for you cannot catch Down's syndrome from a sneeze, a hug, or a handshake! Remember, God made them differently-abled (or you can call them "special"), but they still hope you will call them *friend!*

read and consider...

Ask the question, "What would Jesus do?"
Why did Jesus take time for children?
Do you love and enjoy your brothers and sisters?

Read: Matthew 19:13–15.
1 Peter 3:8: "Finally, be ye all of one mind, having compassion one of another, love as brethren, be pitiful, be courteous."

Shall We Gather at the River

A song often brightens a long, weary day;
How precious to hear a child sing while at play.
Songs comfort the heartbroken, the sorrowing and sad,
With the hope of reunion where all will be glad.

The heat was oppressive in Brooklyn, New York, in the summer of 1865. City life was miserable enough during the intense heat waves of summertime, but now a fierce epidemic was raging through the city. Hundreds had already died, and many more were sick and dying.

For many days, Pastor Robert Lowry unceasingly ministered to the needs of his congregation. He visited the sick, comforted the dying, and gave solace to the many families who were losing loved ones.

One afternoon the pastor returned home in a state of physical exhaustion. The stifling heat pressed around him. As he rested in his home, he recalled how his people often asked, "Pastor, the river of death has parted us. Shall we meet again at the river of life?"

Pastor Lowry had assured his flock over and over that the broken family circles would be complete again at the river of life that flows by the throne of God. He had repeated this promise to hundreds of families as home after home was robed in the dark cloak of sorrow.

The exhausted pastor sat at his little organ to find relief in music from the pent-up emotions of his heart. He thought of "God's precious little angels," the bright innocent children who were taken by the epidemic, and of the adults, friends, and relatives who had gone on before.

He was filled with a heavenly inspiration; the words and music of a new song flowed forth.

Soon he was singing, "Shall we gather at the river, where bright angel feet have trod, with its crystal tide forever, flowing by the throne of God?"

The chorus of the song joyously answered his question. "Yes! we'll gather at the river, the beautiful, the beautiful river, gather with the saints at the river that flows by the throne of God."

read and consider...

Would we look forward to heaven if we had no sorrow here? How does the Bible give us comfort in times of sorrow?

Read Revelation 22:1 and 1 Corinthians 15:19.
Revelation 21:4: "And God shall wipe away all tears from their eyes; and there shall be no more death, neither sorrow, nor crying, neither shall there be any more pain: for the former things are passed away."

The Appointment They Could Not Miss

Dave Swallow lived with his mother in Indiana. He was left alone when she died in 1997. He worried about the possibility of a disaster at the turn of the century. He became obsessed with stocking goods. He bought bags and bags of charcoal briquettes—until he had a ton. Other provisions included 1,000 or more cans of food, kerosene lamps, 30 gallons of lamp oil, 275 candles, 732 cans of pop, and much more!

Dave never got to use his provisions. One morning in July 1999, after enjoying breakfast with a friend, he walked out to his old red pick-up truck. Before he got in, he fell over—dead from a heart attack.

Dave was ready for a crisis, but was he ready to meet God?

* * * * * * *

Monday morning dawned bright and clear. Fannie Schlabach was getting ready for work at Walnut Hills Nursing Home. She always had been on time in the last ten years, except once when a blizzard hindered her.

This morning, Fannie felt ill; then her chest began to hurt terribly. Her sister Katie called 911, but before the ambulance arrived, Fannie had a massive heart attack and was gone. God had planned another appointment for her that day.

Paul Weaver preached at Fannie's funeral. He found Amos 4:12 highlighted in her Bible: "Prepare to meet thy

God." Fannie loved the Lord. She had prepared for her last appointment. Jesus meant much to Fannie in life. He meant everything to her in death.

* * * * * * * * * * *

On a stormy, wintry evening, close to Becks Mill, Ohio, a van load of men was traveling home from work.

After a day of hard labor, what is better than going home? The men thought that the next door they would walk through would be the doors of their own homes, where delicious food awaited them and loving arms would welcome them.

A large tree beside the road swayed and shook in the stormy gale. A huge branch came crashing down and hit the van with a terrible blow. Two of the men, a father and son, Roy and Allen Yoder, never reached home. The next door that opened for them was the door of eternity. Instead of meeting their family that night, they were ushered into eternity.

Many do not prepare for the final call of death, but for Christians we do not need to be afraid when death calls us.

read and consider...

What verse was highlighted in Fannie's Bible?
Whatever happens, look to God.

Read: 1 John 1:9 and Romans 5:8, 9.
Hebrews 9:27: "It is appointed unto men once to die, but after this the judgment."

How Could It Be?

August 19, 1935, was a warm, sunny morning. At the breakfast table John P. Witmer said he was ready to sell some hogs. He asked his children to help him sort out the nice fat ones for the market.

"Race you to the pig pen," Dan hollered, as he and Alberta went out the door. Dad clapped his straw hat on and followed the children at a slower pace.

Soon the pigs were running around the pen. It took patience to get the fat ones into the barn. As they were working, suddenly Dan let out an awful yell and clutched his foot. The hogs were forgotten as everyone ran to Dan, who by now was sitting down, moaning in pain.

Dad quickly saw that Dan had stepped on a rusty old wire. The wire punctured his foot beneath his toe and could be seen from the top of his foot, just under the skin.

Dad was afraid the wire would break off if he tried to pull it out. Quickly he hitched the horse to the buggy, helped Dan in, and at a brisk trot they headed for the doctor's office in Plain City.

Dan's toe hurt so badly that the doctor gave him chloroform to ease the pain. After the wire was removed, the doctor set to work cleaning the wound. Suddenly Dad exclaimed, "Dan is not breathing!" Quickly the doctor worked to revive him, and soon Dan was breathing again.

The doctor went back to work. He had just finished cleaning the foot and was ready to bandage it when Dad saw that again Dan was not breathing. Desperately the doctor tried to revive him, but Dan was gone.

This was a great a shock to the whole family and to their community. Dan had always been a healthy boy, full of life and ambition. How could it be that he had so suddenly left them?

Some folks told Dad, "Sue that doctor; he should have had a nurse helping him. We heard the rumor that the doctor said Dan had a bad heart. We all know that is not the truth."

Dad sadly replied, "That would not bring our boy back. We have had Dr. Holmes as a family doctor for many years. We will leave the matter with God."

John and Martha Witmer grieved the death of their son, Dan.

Dan's death was a stark reminder of the uncertainties of life. It was a summons to "prepare to meet thy God." None of us knows when we will be called home to heaven or when Christ will return.

read and consider...

Is it wise to sue a doctor when he makes a mistake? Why or why not?

Remember Romans 12:18, 19.

Read Romans 12:18, 19 and Psalm 31:15.

2 Samuel 12:23: "I shall go to him, but he shall not return to me."

The Truth Cannot Be Slain

In the olden days, a knight was a fearless, brave hero. The believers referred to martyrs as "ritter" or knights: strong, brave heroes, champions of the truth.

Dark clouds hung over the Haslibach family farm in the Emmental, a picturesque valley framed by the lovely mountains of Switzerland.

The 1500's were dangerous and troubled times for the aged Anabaptist preacher, Hans Haslibacher, and for all those who truly knew and obeyed God. They could not meet freely to worship, but had to meet secretly under the cloak of darkness in the forests or in remote caves. They encouraged each other from the Word of God. They lived out their beliefs, even at the cost of their own lives.

When he was an old man, Hans Haslibacher was caught by the authorities and imprisoned in the city of Bern. There he was tortured severely. No matter what his torturers did to him, Hans would not forsake his God. His testimony was, "My faith I never will forsake, though life and body you should take."

The men in authority told him, "Leave your faith, or a man will strike off your head."

One Saturday night, an angel of God came to Haslibacher in a dream. The angel told him, " 'Tis God who me to thee doth send to comfort thee before thine end. Do not be afraid of the sword; I will stand by you."

The next Monday, the officials came to Haslibacher and told him he must die the next day. That night, he had another vision. He was told that at his death God would send three signs to show he was done an injustice.

Before his death, Haslibacher spoke kindly to his executioner: "Though you take my innocent life," he said, "it is well with my soul. God will show you three signs today.

"1. When my head is struck off, it will fall into my hat and laugh aloud.

"2. The sun will become red as blood.

"3. The town well will give forth blood.

"May God be merciful to those who sentenced me to death."

When he came to the place of execution, Hans took off his hat and laid it before the people. Then, falling on his knees, he prayed the Lord's Prayer, committed his life to his heavenly Father, and bravely faced his death.

The lords and the watching people were struck with fear and awe when the three signs came to pass.

They said, "No more Anabaptist blood will we shed."

The executioner said, " 'Tis guiltless blood I shed today."

Another said, "His mouth did laugh; that surely indicates God's wrath."

Hans Haslibacher was executed for his faith on December 20, 1571. Persecution of the Anabaptists ceased there after his death.

Today one can still visit the Haslibach farm in Switzerland.

Resources: *Martyrs Mirror*, pages 1128-1129 and *Songs of the Ausbund*, pages 347-353.

Why could Hans Haslibacher face death fearlessly?

What can we do to become strong for God?

Read 1 John 2:14, Revelation 19:1, 2, and Psalm 107:1, 2.

Revelation 12:11: "And they overcame him by the blood of the Lamb, and by the word of their testimony; and they loved not their lives unto the death."

Bessie's Roll Call

Jim Black cut through a back alley on his way to the post office in Williamsport, Pennsylvania. Passing a row of shabby houses, he noticed a poorly-clad young girl sweeping the porch of an old house. The girl's face wore lines of worry and neglect.

Jim's heart was full of love for God and mankind; he was concerned for the young girl. He asked her, "Do you attend Sunday school?"

The girl replied, "No sir, I don't have any nice clothes to wear. How I would love to go!"

Jim told his wife about the needy girl. She and some friends were happy to take her some nice clothes and other things that brought joy and thankfulness to the heart of the girl. There was little happiness in her life. Her father was a drunkard who sometimes beat her.

Bessie faithfully began to attend Sunday school and youth meetings. She loved it and wouldn't miss a meeting. Each time the roll call was taken, Bessie was there.

At the evening consecration meetings, the youth answered roll call by giving a Bible verse. One night, Jim Black called Bessie's name, but there was no answer. Again he called her name, but there was only silence.

Jim was troubled. Had Bessie's father forbidden her to come, or had he beaten her? After the service, he hurried to her house. He found Bessie pale and very ill. He called his own doctor. The doctor said Bessie had an advanced case of pneumonia. This was in the 1800's, and pneumonia was often fatal.

Jim walked home with a prayer in his heart for Bessie. He kept thinking about how Bessie had not responded to roll call. It reminded him that someday there would be a roll call in heaven. How awful for those whose names are not written in the Lamb's Book of Life!

Jim was a talented song leader. He searched for a song that would impress upon the youth the great importance of being ready for heaven's roll call. To his disappointment, he found no such song.

A voice in his heart said, "Why don't you write a song about heaven's roll call?" Later the thought came again so strongly that tears filled Jim's eyes. The words seemed to flow from his mind:

When the trumpet of the Lord shall sound,
And time shall be no more;
And the morning breaks eternal bright and fair,
When the saved of earth shall gather over on the other shore,
And the roll is called up yonder, I'll be there.

He wrote the complete set of words and the tune came in the same way. In a few days' time he felt he understood why God had given him that song. His dear little friend Bessie was called home to heaven.

"When the Roll Is Called Up Yonder" was first sung publicly at Bessie's funeral.

The large audience was deeply touched. God had called their Bessie home. In her place, He had given a new song, a great reminder to all of us to be ready when the roll calls us up yonder.

Is there someone you should be inviting to Sunday school?
What did Jim Black do for the Lord?

Read Acts 1:8 and Matthew 28:19, 20.
Revelation 3:5: "He that overcometh, the same shall be clothed
  in white raiment; and I will not blot out his name out of the
  book of life, but I will confess his name before my Father
  and before his angels."

Eighteen Years of This

God is sovereign. He chooses to heal some people here on earth. Others are healed when they gain the heavenly shore. Some are called home suddenly. Others suffer a trial of patience as they lose their strength and need constant care, becoming dependent on others.

Whatever comes we can trust in the sovereignty of God!

Owen Schrock was in his sixties. He was happiest when he was busy. On a lovely day he was on his tractor plowing in the field. As he was driving in from the field, he felt something strange come over him. He stopped the tractor, but he could not get off alone. He had had a spinal stroke and could not walk!

Owen took therapy. He had an intense desire to walk again. But he had to wait 18 years for the fulfillment of that desire. Eighteen years later, God called him home.

At his funeral, the minister said, "Owen likely does not remember all those wheelchair days now."

What a glad thought that in heaven there will be no more wheelchairs. There will be no more trials of patience, no more long, dreary days. In heaven, all will be sunshine and gladness.

read and consider...

What can cheer us amid our trials?
Do we really believe that God's way is best?
Read Romans 8:28 and Romans 8:18.
Revelation 21:4: "And God shall wipe away all tears from their eyes; and there shall be no more death, neither sorrow, nor crying, neither shall there be any more pain; for the former things are passed away."

Coals of Fire and Courage

Am I My Brother's Keeper?

He stood at the crossroad all alone,

With the sunrise in His face;

He had no fear for the path unknown,

He was set for a manly race.

But the road stretched east and the road stretched west;

There was no one to tell him which way was best;

So my chum turned wrong and went down, down, down,

Till he lost the race and the victor's crown,

And fell at last in an ugly snare,

Because no one stood at the crossroad there.

Another chum on another day,
At the selfsame crossroads stood;
He paused a moment to choose the way
That would lead to the greater good.
And the road stretched east and the road stretched west;
But I was there to show him the best;
So my chum turned right and went on and on,
Till he won the race and the victor's crown;
He came at last to the mansion fair,
Because I stood at the crossroads there.

Since then I have raised a daily prayer,
That I be kept faithfully standing there,
To warn the runners as they come,
And save my own and another's chum.

—Sadie Tiller Crawley

A Rose for His Enemy

During his life, Pastor Richard Wurmbrand shared many unusual stories from his difficult years in prisons. Here is one of those stories.

A new prisoner was shoved into our cell in Romania. He was shorn, thin and dirty, just like we all were. At first, no one recognized the new unfortunate man. But then someone exclaimed, "This is Captain Propescu!"

We all knew about this man! He had been one of the worst torturers of Christians. We did not draw back from him. We asked how he came to be among us in our miserable cell?

In tears he said, "One day as I sat in my office, a boy entered with a beautiful flower in his hand. I guessed him to be about 12 years old. He told me his name and explained to me why he came.

" 'Today is my mother's birthday, Captain Popescu. You are the one that arrested my mother. I was in the habit of bringing her a flower on her birthday. I cannot give her one today because of you. Instead, I decided to bring a flower to the mother of your children. Take this flower to your wife and tell her of my love. My own dear mother is a Christian who taught us to love our enemies, to reward their evil with good.'

"My hard, wicked heart was broken. I embraced the lad and knew I could no longer torture God's people. I was no longer any good as a communist police officer. That is why I am thrown in with you today."

Captain Popescu was ruined as a communist police officer, but through the actions of a small boy who was armed with the powerful weapon of love, he accepted Christ's love and eternal hope. The persecutor was now persecuted and a brother in the faith!

Who can comprehend the greatness of the love of God in the heart of a 12-year-old that prompted and enabled him to give such a touching gift of love? Who can ever underestimate the power of love?

Resource: *The Voice of the Martyrs*, September, 2004.

read and consider...

How much more our homes would be blessed if we learned in daily life to return kindness for petty rudeness!

How does God want you to show kindness today?

Is someone at church or school mean to you? What could you do for them in return?

A little proverb goes: "You can catch more flies with honey than with vinegar."

Read Romans 12:18-20.

Matthew 5:44-45: "But I say unto you, Love your enemies, bless them that curse you, do good to them that hate you, and pray for them which despitefully use you, and persecute you; that ye may be the children of your Father which is in heaven."

Lanterns, Torches, and Weapons

It was a beautiful, clear evening. Jesus and His disciples went to the Mount of Olives. It was peaceful among the old trees, but there was no relaxation for Jesus that awful night. "My soul is overwhelmed to the point of death," He said. He told the disciples to watch and pray. But their eyes were heavy, and they slept while He fell to the ground and poured out His heart to His Father. At last, He committed His spirit into the hands of the Father.

Through the olive grove came the sound of an approaching mob. It was a mob of strong, hate-filled men carrying lanterns, torches, and weapons. They came in the darkness with their puny lights to capture Jesus, the father of lights, the light of the world, the maker of the sun, moon, and stars. Jesus, the maker and master of mankind.

Jesus fearlessly went forth to meet the mob. "Who are you looking for?" He asked. They replied, "Jesus of Nazareth." "I am He," Jesus calmly responded. When he said that, the mob of strong men staggered backward and fell to the ground.

Judas came then to give Jesus a kiss, that awful kiss of betrayal. "Friend, do what you came for," Jesus said. "How can you betray the Messiah with a kiss?"

When the disciples saw what was taking place, they exclaimed, "Master, shall we fight?"

Impulsive Peter didn't wait for orders. He grabbed his sword and slashed at Malchus, the high priest's servant, lopping off his ear.

"Enough of that," said Jesus. "Put your sword away. Don't you realize I could call my Father, and he would send thousands of angels to protect us?" Jesus then touched the servant's ear and the severed ear was restored! Imagine, even when Jesus was being betrayed, he cared about others!

Then Jesus told the mob, "This is your hour, when darkness reigns." They seized Him and led Him away to be tried, condemned, and crucified.

His disciples all forsook Him and fled.

Jesus, wonderful Savior! He came to minister. He came to GIVE his life a ransom for many.

read and consider...

Why did the mob come in the darkness to take Jesus?
Why didn't Jesus call ten thousand angels to protect him?

Read: Luke 22:39–46.
Psalm 91:2: "I will say of the LORD, He is my refuge and my
fortress: my God; in Him will I trust."

Good Will Triumph

High in the picturesque mountains of Austria is a sturdy old castle. It is an intriguing place, full of stories and history.

In the depths of the castle is a damp, chilly dungeon. Four hundred and fifty years ago, two Anabaptists were imprisoned there. The hapless men had been traveling through the village in the valley below and stopped to eat at an inn. Reverently, unashamedly, they had bowed their heads to thank the Lord for the food.

The sharp eyes of men who hated the believers saw them praying. They were apprehended and thrown into the dungeon.

God knows how long they languished in that dismal place. God knows those who truly love and honor Him and God will reward them.

Hundreds of years later, during World War II, the German army demanded the rights to the castle and used it for their headquarters. They always took the best for themselves. But where are they today? What is the reward for all of their ungodly deeds?

Today, this same old castle, Schloss Mittersill, is a Christian retreat center and a place of lodging where travelers can find rest and refreshment.

I was with a group who went down the winding stairs into that dungeon and sang triumphantly, "Faith of our fathers living still . . .we will be true to thee till death."

On that lovely Sunday morning, we held a service of praise in a thick stone-walled chapel at Schloss Mittersill.

The joyful songs of praise echoed in the lovely old chapel. We experienced a foretaste of heaven.

Would you be courageous enough to pray in public even if it
     might cost you imprisonment?
What is the reward for faithfulness to God?
If you want to praise God in eternity, start today.

Read Mark 8:36 and Romans 1:16.
Acts 27:35: "And when he had thus spoken, he took bread, and
     gave thanks to God in presence of them all."

Such a Sweet Aroma!

What would it be like to be 86 years old?

Imagine having the privilege of sitting at the feet of the Apostle John, the disciple of Jesus, and being taught by him.

"Polycarp, Polycarp," the old man's friend gasped, terror filling his eyes, "you must hide, the soldiers are even now searching for you. The mob is crying, *death to the Christians,* and now they want you, our leader!"

Polycarp was hurried away and hidden at a farm in the country.

Polycarp, the respected 86-year-old bishop of Smyrna, was not afraid of death. Only recently he had dreamed that his couch was ablaze. His thoughts went to the many believers who had died at the stake in the burning fires. He had a premonition that his days were numbered. The soldiers were fast nearing his hiding place, and Polycarp did not wish to flee again.

With gracious kindness he welcomed the men who wished to capture him. He set a feast before them and invited them to eat. He requested an hour to pray while the men partook of the food.

He poured out his heart to the Father, imploring God for strength in the hour of death. He prayed for all the sheep of the church of Smyrna.

Some of his captors were troubled at arresting such a kindly old man. "We would not have had to make such haste for an aged man such as he," one remarked.

Polycarp was given a mule to ride into the city. On the way, some of the royalty met up with him and cordially welcomed him into their carriage. They besought him with kind, flattering words to give up the faith. They seemed to show respect for his age.

"Why not offer sacrifice and incense before the Lord Emperor and save your life?" they pleaded. At first Polycarp kept silent, but when they demanded of him an answer, he said, "I shall never do what you request and counsel me to do."

When the men saw that Polycarp was unmovable in his faith, they mocked and jeered him, and violently shoved him out of their carriage.

Polycarp was led to the amphitheater. A voice came to him from heaven saying, "Be strong, O Polycarp! And valiant in thy confession and in the suffering that awaits thee."

In spite of the great commotion, other Christians also heard the voice and they, with Polycarp, were strengthened.

The Roman proconsul endeavored to show respect to the aged bishop. He urged him to change his mind and renounce Christ.

But Polycarp stood firm. "I have now served my Lord Christ Jesus 86 years. He never did me any wrong. How can I deny my King who hath hitherto preserved me from all evil and redeemed me?" he candidly replied.

When threatened with death by wild beasts or by fire, Polycarp calmly affirmed, "Thou shalt not by either of them move me to deny my Lord. Your fire burns for an hour and goes out, but the fire of the coming judgment of God is eternal."

And so the aged bishop was tied to the stake. He prayed passionately, thanking God that he was considered worthy to partake in the sufferings of Christ and imploring God to receive his life as an offering.

As soon as he said "Amen," a raging hot fire was lit. Yet, to the astonishment of all, as the flames leaped high around him, Polycarp was not consumed. Eyewitnesses said, "We smelled such a sweet aroma, as the breath of incense or some precious spice."

The executioner was commanded to pierce him with a sword. His blood flowed out and the hot fire was quenched.

Thus Polycarp, the faithful witness of Jesus Christ, entered into the rest of the saints. He may have been the last living link with the apostolic church, as tradition states that he studied with the Apostle John.

Many of the children of God were strengthened in their faith by the life and death of Polycarp, who gave his all and his best. In life and in death he was a living sacrifice for God!

Resources: *Foxes Book of Martyrs, The 100 Most Important Events in Christian History,* and *The Martyrs Mirror.*

read and consider...

Can you say, "Come what may, I will be true to Christ"?
What was the message Polycarp heard when he entered the arena?

Read Romans 12:1 and Matthew 10:28.
John 16:33: "These things have I spoken unto you, that in me ye might have peace. In the world ye shall have tribulation; but be of good cheer; I have overcome the world."

You Need Jesus!

Scotty had a tool sharpening and key making business in Scotland. He was a good worker, but he was in trouble at home. His unhappy wife was threatening to leave him because Scotty loved to drink. Not only that, his son was beginning to follow him to the bars!

One day Scotty poured out his troubles to a Christian friend. "What should I do?" he cried. "How can I stop drinking? Should I try Alcoholics Anonymous? Where can I go for help?"

"You need a person—a Savior," his friend replied. "You need forgiveness and pardon. The fellowship of others is good, but you need Jesus. You need to become a new man. You must be born again. Jesus can help you. He can take away that awful desire for drink!"

"But how is this possible?" Scotty asked.

"You must tell Jesus, the One who can bear your burdens and cleanse you from all sin. There will always be problems in this life, but Jesus longs to be your Savior and friend. He is always ready to hear, always ready to forgive."

Some weeks after Scotty and his friend had prayer together in his shop, two men called on Scotty. They asked him if he wanted to make some money. "That is why I am in business," Scotty retorted. "What can I do for you men?"

The men told Scotty that the business he was doing was peanuts. "We can give you 5,000 pounds for 15 minutes of work," they bribed. "All we want you to do is to make a duplicate set of two keys from a nearby bank. At noon, when all the other employees are out for lunch, we will bring you the keys. If you work fast, we will have the original keys back at the bank before anyone misses them. Would you like to earn that much so easily?"

By the power of God, Scotty told them to get packing and never come back!

Later, Scotty related the happening to his Christian friend. "If it had not been for God's help, I could not have resisted that offer. Thank God, He has also helped me not to touch a drop of liquor since the day you prayed with me."

Hallelujah! What a Savior! No matter what temptation the devil shoots your way, Jesus can help you—Jesus alone. How true are the lovely words of the hymn, "I Must Tell Jesus."

> Oh how the world to evil allures me!
> Oh how my heart is tempted to sin!
> I must tell Jesus, and He will help me
> Over the world the victory to win.

read and consider...

Who did Scotty need to help him conquer the demon of drink?
How did he have strength to resist the offer of quick and easy
money?
How can you find strength and power to do the will of God?

Read Ephesians 6:10–16.
I John 1:9: "If we confess our sins, he is faithful and just to
forgive us our sins, and to cleanse us from all unrighteous-
ness."

Home Run to Heaven

Billy Sunday was a powerful evangelist in the early 1900's. When Billy preached, he did not just stand there; no sir, he jumped, ran, and slid across the platform. At times, he would lean out so far that folks were afraid he would fall off the platform. It is said that through his ministry 300,000 people were led to faith in Christ!!

At a young age, Billy was sent off to a boarding school. His father died in World War I. His mother was too poor to provide for her two sons. At the boarding school, Billy's love for sports grew. Later he began to play professional baseball. Once, when he was playing left field, he ran back to catch a fly, only to discover that the ball was going over the fence. Instead of giving up, he ran toward the fence and vaulted over it. He reached out his arm and caught the ball!

One night in Chicago, a Pacific Garden Mission worker invited the ball players to the mission. That night Billy gave his heart to the Lord. He quit drinking, gambling, and smoking. His teammates could plainly see he was changed! He asked for a contract in which he would not play ball on Sundays, and it was granted. As he traveled with his team, he frequently gave talks about his conversion.

On September 5, 1888, he married Nell Tompson. After a number of years, Billy felt God was telling him to quit playing baseball and go into full time Christian ministry. Nell encouraged him to do so, even though the decision to work for the Lord cut their income to one sixth of what it had been!

When Billy Sunday preached, no one slept. Once, when giving the invitation, he leaped up onto the pulpit, stretched out his arms, and pled with the people to repent.

Billy hated the evils of liquor. Bartenders in New York City heard how Billy was getting people to shut down bars. When they heard Billy was coming to New York City, they raised $100,000 to stop him. But Billy came into the city and preached against liquor harder than ever.

In 1933, Billy was still preaching when he had a heart attack. His song leader gave the invitation. Billy leaned on the pulpit for support, and many responded that night.

Shortly before his death two years later, Billy wrote, "I care not what is said about me. . . . I am and always have been plain Billy Sunday, trying to do God's will in preaching Jesus and Him crucified and arisen from the dead for our sins."

Billy had played baseball with all his might. He traded that for preaching for Jesus with all his might.

read and consider...

Why was Billy willing to preach even though he couldn't earn as
  much preaching as he could playing ball?
Why did Billy not want to play ball on Sunday anymore?

Read 2 Timothy 4:5–8.
Colossians 3:23, 24: "And whatsoever ye do, do it heartily, as
  to the Lord, and not unto men; Knowing that of the Lord ye
  shall receive the reward of the inheritance: for ye serve the
  Lord Christ."

Running to Win

Eric Liddell and his friends eagerly scanned the 1924 Olympic timetable to see what days and times the sporting events were held. Eric searched for the 100 meter race, his best event. Suddenly he turned pale and quietly announced to his teammates, "I can't run."

"Can't run? Hey what's the problem, man, what do you mean?"

"I don't run on Sundays," Eric stated. "For me, Sunday is a day to worship God, not a day for sports."

"Whatever is wrong with Eric that he won't run the race on Sunday?" the people scoffed. Newspapers scolded and criticized. "He's just trying to get more attention!" they wrote. One British nobleman was quoted as saying, "To play the game is the only thing in life that matters."

"Tom," Eric addressed his longtime friend and trainer, "do you really want to know why I can't run? God's fourth commandment to Moses said, 'Remember the Sabbath day to keep it holy.' I am not remembering God's Sabbath if I run in a race that honors me on that day. I will not ignore one of God's commands. I love God too much."

Tom sighed. He knew Eric well enough to know he would not change his mind or waver in his convictions, not even for the Olympics.

Though the 400 meter race was not his best event, Eric began training for it because it was not held on Sunday. God meant more, much more, to Eric than an Olympic gold medal.

Years earlier when Eric was only five, he stayed with his brother at a Scottish boarding school while their parents returned to China. The separation was hard on all of them, yet the boys adjusted and did well at school.

The Liddel brothers enjoyed all sorts of track events. Running was Eric's favorite sport. Sometimes his parents wondered whether God or sports would be most important to Eric. Eric never forgot the advice his father had given him years earlier. "What matters, Eric, is how you run the race of life. Winning a medal is not so important. Paul wrote to the church at Corinth, 'run in such a way to get a prize,' and what prize does that mean?"

"The prize of heaven, Father," Eric stoutly responded.

Yes, indeed, Eric loved to run. But his heart was set on the heavenly prize! When older, he attended Bible studies regularly. He visited the sick at a nearby mission. He tried to be a friend to all the boys at school.   Finally, it was the week of the Olympics, July 1924. On Sunday, when the race Eric had trained for was run, Eric was speaking at a church about his commitment to Christ.

On the morning of July 6, the day Eric would run the 400 meter race, an older man handed Eric a note. Eric stuck it in his pocket.

Hours later he pulled it out. The note read, "In the old book it says, 'Them that honor me, I will honor.' Wishing you the best of success always."

Eric bowed his head and whispered, "Thank you, God." He was greatly encouraged!

That day, Eric not only won the 400 meter race, he also set a world record of 47.6 seconds.

The same press that had booed him now praised him. Scotland had a new hero! Eric left the stadium as quickly and quietly as he could after the race, for he was working on another speech he planned to give on Sunday.

Eric was an Olympic champion, yet he remembered that others who had run fast, hard and well, had not come in first. Respectfully, he said, "In the dust of defeat, as well as in the laurels of victory, there is a glory to be found if one has done his best."

Everyone was surprised when a year later Eric announced he was going to join his family in China. He was preparing for a greater race, a race in which he would give his all, his best, and eventually his life!

Eric was God's missionary in China for 20 years. On February 2, 1945, Eric's last race was run. He died of a brain tumor in a Japanese prison camp just months before World War II ended. He left a wife and three daughters and a legacy of strong faith and sacrificial service to Jesus Christ—the one who was always the center of his life.

"Those who love God never say goodbye for the last time," was Eric's testimony.

Do you want to be inspired and challenged? Read books about Eric Liddell.

read and consider...

Who do you chose to honor on Sunday?
If you had been Eric, what would your choice have been?

Read: I Samuel 2:30 and Romans 1:16.
Joshua 24:15: "Choose you this day whom ye will serve. . . . as for me and my house, we will serve the Lord."

God Owns It All

Pablo and Eunice Yoder are missionaries in war-torn Nicaragua where robbery is a huge temptation to the poor natives. Pablo's family has been robbed many times.

One morning, Tim Schrock, the bishop of their church, came to Pablo's house. "Pablo," he said, "we went through our house this morning and gave everything to the Lord; I think you should do that too."

After Pablo considered the matter, he called his family together. They experienced such a blessing and peace by praying, "Lord, it is all yours: the farm, the cows, the calves, the sewing machine. Everything, Lord, all is yours!"

Out of the blue one morning, Pablo discovered that the two calves were gone. The one calf was Pablo's and the other calf he had been keeping in his pasture for a poor lady from their church. The robbers had hit yet again!

The Lord had been working in Pablo's heart. Now he prayed, "Lord, the calves are yours."

Pablo talked to the mother of the woman who owned the calf. The lady said, "My daughter has decided to leave it in God's hands. God knows where the calves are. They are His anyway. If it is His will, we will get them back!"

Pablo was amazed and blessed by their attitude. "Those people are so poor they struggle to buy groceries, and yet they can trust God like that!"

A week later, a fellow came and told Pablo he knew where the calves were. He had stolen them himself. He wanted some easy money. This young man was just beginning to steal. The police had already found out, and the man had signed a confession. Now he told Pablo, "The calves are sold and far away. I want to settle up with you; I want to make things right."

Pablo was grateful for the opportunity to witness to this young man and give him some neighborly advice. The man paid Pablo for his calf, though the money didn't quite cover its worth.

The amazing thing was how the Lord greatly blessed the sister who owned the other calf. The former robber wanted to replace her stolen calf. He gave her a big steer, worth more than the one he had stolen!

"The whole experience was a tremendous blessing," said Pablo. "It makes the biggest difference if what you have belongs to the Lord."

read and consider...

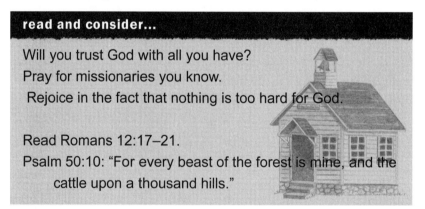

Will you trust God with all you have?
Pray for missionaries you know.
 Rejoice in the fact that nothing is too hard for God.

Read Romans 12:17–21.
Psalm 50:10: "For every beast of the forest is mine, and the cattle upon a thousand hills."

chapter seven

Faithfulness
Your Place

Is your place a large place?
Guard it with care,
He set you there.

Is your place a small place?
Tend it with care,
He set you there.

Whatever your place,
It is not yours alone,
But His who set you there.

—John Oxenham

Wanted!

1. Fathers like Abraham. "He will command his children and his household after him, and they shall keep the way of the Lord." (Genesis 18:19)

2. Mothers like Hannah. "As long as he [her son] liveth, he shall be lent to the Lord."
(1 Samuel 1:28)

3. Boys like Jesus. He returned with His parents to Nazareth, "and was subject unto them." (Luke 2:51)

4. Girls like the little maid who told her mistress that God could heal Naaman's leprosy. (2 Kings 5:1-3)

5. Brothers like Nehemiah and Hanani who served God together. (Nehemiah 7:2)

6. Sisters like Mary and Martha who received Jesus into their home and into their lives. (Luke 10:38, 39)

7. Men in high places like Daniel in whom no fault could be found. (Daniel 6:5)

8. Preachers like Paul who "in weakness, and in fear, and in much trembling" presented the truth in the power of the Spirit. (1 Corinthians 2:1-5)

9. Servants of God like Barnabas. "He was a good man, and full of the Holy Ghost and of faith." (Acts 11:24)

10. Lovers of the Bible like the Bereans. "They received the word with all readiness of mind, and searched the scriptures daily." (Acts 17:11)

—Source Unknown

Faithful or Famous?

Have you ever seen the incredible beauty of Niagara Falls?

Father Hennepin who viewed the falls in 1678 said the falls have no equal.

The waters of Niagara Falls plunge down from a height of more than 500 feet. The falls are composed of two sheets of water and a cascade. In the midst, these waters foam and boil in a fearful manner.

The meaning of the word Niagara is "the straight" and "thundering waters."

Millions of people go each year to view Niagara Falls. The beauty of the waters are a tribute to the awesome handiwork and power of God almighty.

Many, many people gaze at the falls but, sadly, all do not see the hand of God there.

In 1901, Annie Taylor, a schoolteacher from Michigan, stood at the falls. Instead of marveling at God's creation, her mind was forming an idea of how she could become famous.

Could I, would I dare to get into a big wooden barrel, with a large soft cushion and my black cat? We could float downstream, plunge over the falls, and then be rescued grandly in the river below. I could make a name for myself and always be remembered for such a daring deed! Why not, indeed! Why not try it?

Annie found some men and newspaper reporters to assist her in her scheme. She told them she was 43 years of age. Later records confirm that she was actually 63 years old! Annie was strapped in her barrel in a special harness, towed out into the Niagara River, and let loose. The little barrel holding Annie Taylor plunged over that 500 foot height. Seventeen minutes later her barrel drifted close to the Canadian shore, and she was rescued!

Dazed, but successful, Annie said, "No one ought *ever* do that again." Desperately she had sought for fame and found it by conquering the mighty Falls of Niagara. Yet her fame brought with it no real satisfaction or peace. Twenty years later, Annie died destitute in Niagara Falls, New York.

read and consider...

For what reason did God create man?
What is the most important thing in life?

Read John 3:16 and Hebrews 12:28.
Revelation 2:10: "Be thou faithful unto death, and I will give thee a crown of life."

God Gives a Song

Life is a mixture of sunshine and storms. Whatever happens, we need to remember: God always loves us, God always cares about us, and God is always with us.

"I am so thankful and happy we can finally begin building our own house," George's wife told him.

"Yes, dear, all praise to God, He is the maker and giver of every good thing!" George warmly responded.

George A. Young was a simple country preacher and a carpenter. His salary was small, and his life was not easy. But George and his wife were rich in their love and loyalty toward God and each other.

Their family worked hard, all lending a helping hand. The walls of the house went up and finally the roof was put on. It was an eventful day when they moved into their new house.

George was called to hold meetings in another area. He willingly went. His ambition in life was to give his best for God. But while he was away, a rough group of men, who did not like the preacher or the preacher's God and Gospel, went to his new house and set it on fire. Red hot flames soon leaped upward, brightening the night sky for miles around. The evil deed left nothing but a heap of smoldering ashes.

Imagine the deep hurt and disappointment of George and his family as they viewed the ruin of the home that was dear to them, the house they had worked so hard to build.

It is thought that after this great disaster, George penned the verses of the faith-filled hymn, *God Leads Us Along*.

In shady green pastures, so rich and so sweet,
God leads His dear children along.
Where the waters cool flow bathes the weary one's feet,
God leads His dear children along.

Sometimes on the mount where the sun shines so bright,
God leads His dear children along.
Sometimes in the valley in the darkest of night,
God leads His dear children along.

Though sorrows befall us and Satan oppose,
God leads His dear children along.
Through grace we can conquer, defeat all our foes;
God leads his dear children along.

Chorus: Some through the waters, some through the
        flood,
Some through the fire, but all through the blood.
Some through great sorrows, but God gives a song,
In the night season and all the day long.

read and consider...

George and his wife were rich in what is most important. What were those true riches?

Why does keeping heaven as our goal help us through the difficult times in life?

Read: Psalm 9:9 and Psalm 31:15.

Philippians 4:19: "But my God shall supply all your need according to his riches in glory by Christ Jesus."

Make Lemonade

Gerald Yoder and his family are missionaries to Indians in Kenora, Ontario. Gerald once said, "When I was a boy, a poster on my bedroom wall had this message, "When life gives you lemons, make lemonade." What a nice way to say, "Make the best out of life's difficulties."

"Lately I have run into some real lemons," Gerald said. "I took my car to a local garage for minor repairs. A man I guessed to be in his sixties came into the office spouting more 'Christ,' 'God,' and 'hell' words than I used in last Sunday's sermon.

"As soon as I had the opportunity, I laid my hand on his shoulder, looked him in the eye, and asked him if he realized that he was degrading the name of my God? The man ducked out from under my hand and fled out the door mumbling, 'Don't preach to me, man!' I've never seen an office clear so quickly; like cockroaches fleeing for cover when exposed by light. But the secretary had no excuse to flee. She sat there embarrassed, her face crimson. She apologized for the speech of all those in the room just seconds before, herself included. I assured her that she need not apologize to me, but that it would be very appropriate for her to repent and ask forgiveness of God for her words, as well as for all her sins.

"I left that place with my heart thumping, wondering what and how I could have said something with totally different results. I felt someone else could have done much better. I did not feel I had handled the situation well. Yet, I knew I would have felt much worse had I not said anything. At any rate, God knew how to get those people on my prayer list.

"Awhile back, I had just opened the worship service we were having on an Indian reserve when a 'lemon' by the name of Frank walked in. I had been preaching for five minutes on the church being in one place in one accord from Acts chapter 1.

"Frank became agitated, stomped up to me, and began asking questions in a loud, angry voice. He stood five feet in front of me. I would have been glad to answer him, but he didn't give me speaking space. He ranted and raved around the room, slamming chairs into each other, boxing the wall, and talking about a gun he had at home.

"I realize I was slow, but I finally found my tongue and calmly, yet with authority, said, 'In the name of Jesus, Frank, I command you to leave this building!'

"Frank stopped his tirade, looked at me, picked up his coat and left. I breathed, thank you, Lord!"

Missionaries need our prayers as they work with many needy "lemons."

read and consider...

What do you do if you hear someone swearing?
Can others tell that you love Jesus?

Read Proverbs 18:10 and Philippians 2:10.
I John 4:4: "Ye are of God, little children, and have overcome them: because greater is he that is in you, than he that is in the world."

Christopher Dock, the Humble Teacher

Blessed be the humble teacher who,
Without any chance for the great rewards of fame
or money,
Renders noble service
And leaves the impress of a genuine and generous
character
In one little corner of the world.
—Edward Eggleston, 1892

Christopher Dock was a devoted teacher and did a noble work for 40 years in the obscurity of the Pennsylvania back country. He felt called by God to teach, and to this great calling he dedicated his life.

There were no public schools in Pennsylvania in the 1700s. The education of children was the responsibility of parents and the church. The main goal of education was to teach children to read the Scriptures and to lead a godly life.

Christopher Dock walked with God. He said, "I have early discovered that if I wish to pursue the calling to teach, I must daily lift up my eyes to God for help." He prayed often that God might help him do the best things for his students.

He opened each school day with worship. He cared deeply about and prayed daily for each student under his instruction. And after they were long gone from his classroom, he wrote letters to his students, urging them to give themselves to God.

Dock's friends urged him to put his teaching methods into writing. He was hesitant to do so, as he felt it would be sinful to encourage his own praise. He wanted to make sure that anything of value in his own writings would be accredited to the blessing and wisdom of God.

It was autumn 1771. The woods were dressed in the season's splendor. Colorful leaves fringed the clearing where a small one-room log schoolhouse stood. The pupils had gone home. In the quiet peacefulness, Dock was setting the schoolroom in order and preparing lessons for the next day.

He opened his roll book and knelt at his desk, as was his daily habit, to pray for each of his students by name. While he was thus talking with his maker, his spirit returned to God. His head dropped, and he slumped to the floor. What a peaceful benediction to his life of dedication and godliness.

When Dock did not return to the farm family where he lodged, his host went to search for him. He went all the way to the little school, and there he found the beloved schoolmaster whose spirit had fled.

The news spread that the schoolmaster had been called home. That week, a somber group of parents and children gathered to show their last respects to the teacher who had meant so much to them.

In God's grace and tender blessing,
All is safe and of much avail;
But without His help and succor
All men's efforts will but fail.
                        —Christopher Dock

Approximately how long did Christopher Dock teach school? Why did he pray for his students each day?

Read Deuteronomy 6:5–7.
Acts 13:36: "For David, after he had served his own generation by the will of God, fell on sleep."

Rules for Children

Christopher Dock wrote "A Hundred Necessary Rules for the Conduct of Children." These rules show us that Dock was a man of noble character and true conviction. His rules were for the morning, for the evening, for meals, and for the conduct of a child at school. There were rules for the conduct of a child on the street, at church, and general rules of conduct. He also wrote "A Hundred Christian Rules for Children."

For your pleasure and edification, here are the first 12 of the 100 rules for children. Included also is the 100th rule from both sets.

Rules for the Conduct of a Child
in the House of His Parents

A. In the morning, during and after rising:
1. Dear child, as soon as you are called in the morning, arise; indeed, accustom yourself to "awaken" at the proper time without being called, and to rise without loitering.
2. When you have left your bed, turn back the covers.
3. Let your first thoughts be turned toward God, after the example of David, who (Psalm 139:18) saith: "When I awake, I am still with thee," and (Psalm 63:6) "I remember thee upon my bed, and meditate on thee in the night watches."
4. Bid a good morning to those whom you meet first and to your parents, sisters, and brothers; not from mere habit, but do it out of true love.
5. Accustom yourself to dress quickly, but at the same time neatly.

6. Instead of idle talk with your sisters and brothers, seek while dressing to have good thoughts. Remember the garb of righteousness in Jesus that has come to you through Jesus, and resolve this day not to sully it by deliberate sinning.

7. When you wash your face and hands, do not splash water about the room.

8. Rinsing the mouth with water each morning and rubbing the teeth with the fingers serves to preserve the teeth.

9. In combing your hair do not stand in the middle of the room, but in a corner.

10. Your morning prayer should be said, not as a matter of an indifferent habit, but in fervent gratitude to God, who has guarded you during the night; pray Him humbly to bless your actions this day; neither forget to sing, and to read the Bible.

11. Do not eat your breakfast on the street or in school; but ask your parents to give it to you at home.

12. Then gather up your books and come to school in proper time.

100. Whatever you see in other Christian people that is good and proper, let it serve you as a model. If there be any virtue and if there be any praise, think on these things (Philippians 4:8).

100. Fear not death, for if thou hast lived a Christian life, thou canst die blessed and happy.

read and consider...

Do you think these rules could be some good goals for your life? Why or why not?

Look up some of the Scripture references mentioned in the rules.

One Million Vehicles

"Yes," Silvia mused, "yes, I do want to take the load of Bibles into the Soviet Union. I know it is dangerous; I know I could get caught. I could be put into prison, tortured, maybe even put to death. But I feel God wants me to take the risk. This is a work for God that needs to be done. I can sense God leading and telling me to pray." And so, Silvia prayed and prayed.

"You cannot go on this dangerous mission," Silvia's friends told her. "You will never get through the border with a load of Bibles." Silvia always calmly responded, "Pray. Pray with me; pray for me."

It was 1983. Silvia prayed. Her friends prayed. The churches were praying. If God wanted those Bibles in the Soviet Union, He would get them there. Finally the day came to leave. The Bibles had come from Austria. The vehicle was loaded with the precious Word of Life. Prayers were constantly ascending to the throne of God as the car rolled down the road.

At the border, Silvia waited in a long line of vehicles. She prayed. She waited. Slowly, slowly she inched her way up to the border. Finally it was Silvia's turn to go through. But alas, many guards came up and told her to pull to the side. Silvia complied and waited and prayed some more.

Presently, a group of guards and the media came up to Silvia's car and made this announcement. "This is the millionth vehicle to cross this border. It will not be opened or searched. You may proceed through unchecked. Welcome to Ukraine!"

What a miracle! What an awesome answer to prayer! God positioned that load of Bibles in just the right place at just the right time!

God rewarded Silvia's faith. She had assurance and peace that this was God's will, and God saw her safely through!

Resource: Master's International newsletter, May, 2005.

Resource: Master's International newsletter, May, 2005.

read and consider...

May you have the courage and faith to do what you know God is leading you to do.

Why was Silvia's car allowed to cross the border without being searched?

Read: Psalm 32:6-8.

Isaiah 41:10: "Fear thou not; for I am with thee: be not dismayed; for I am thy God: I will strengthen thee; yea, I will help thee; yea, I will uphold thee with the right hand of my righteousness."

George Washington Carver

From Poverty to Professor

The small, black baby was sleeping peacefully beside his mother. Suddenly, the quietness of the dark night was shattered by pounding hoofs. The door burst open. The mother and her baby were stolen away, kidnapped by "night raiders" in the deep south in 1864.

The young woman was never seen again, but the tiny baby, George, was found and brought back to his mother's owners, the Carvers.

Susan Carver was a kind and gentle lady. She did all she could to nurse the thin, sickly baby back to health. As soon as he was old enough, she taught him to be handy around the house. She also kindly taught the frail child to sew and knit.

Young George was keenly interested in plants and flowers. He loved all growing things. He would sometimes fall asleep with a bunch of blossoms in his hand. At times, he'd smuggle frogs, toads, or other creeping things into his bedroom. He always wanted to know the name of every stone, flower, or insect.

George greatly longed to go to school. The nearest school for black boys was eight miles away. He begged and pleaded so much that finally, when he was 11 years old, the Carvers consented. Tears ran down Susan's cheeks as she waved good-bye.

It was late that evening when George reached the school. He sat on a pile of logs nearby. His stomach growled. He felt lonely and forsaken, but his desire for an education kept him there.

Thank God that a kindhearted black lady, Mrs. Watkins, took pity on George. She not only gave him supper, she also gave him a home for as long as he attended school in her town. George was delighted to help with the laundry and keep the yard raked and the chickens fed to pay for his room and board.

Best of all, George attended church with the Watkins. Mrs. Watkins (or Aunt Mariah, as George called her) taught him of Jesus, the children's friend. She taught him how to pray and to love the Bible. As soon as George could read, he read the best of all books.

On Christmas Day, Aunt Mariah gave George a special treasure—a small black Bible. He loved to read it. Within the year, George had memorized large segments from Genesis, Psalms, Proverbs, and the Gospels. The Word of God guided his life. When George was nearly 80 years old, he was still reading that same Bible daily!

With much hard work and diligence, George overcame poverty and racism. When treated rudely, he gave kindness in return. He became a brilliant scientist and professor, winning international fame for his agricultural research. He loved helping his people, teaching poor farmers how to grow better crops and how to save money. His goal was not wealth but service to whomever needed him!

Thomas Edison, the famous inventor, offered George W. Carver $50,000 a year if he would work for him. Henry Ford would have given him large sums of money, if he only would come to Dearborn, Michigan. But George refused them both.

Dr. George Washington Carver led a long and useful life. He said, "It has always been the one great goal of my life to be of the greatest good to the greatest number of people possible."

CHAPTER 8

Your Words
Honey Please

Whenever I meet up with bees
I keep quite still and quiet.
For even though I know that these
Add honey to my diet,
It isn't just the nicest thing
Whenever they decide to sting.

Whenever friends meet up with me
I dip my words in honey.
I want to help their day
Be a happy one and sunny,
And words can be the nicest things
When filled with love
And not with stings.
– Author Unknown

*The author received a copy of this poem
from her mother many years ago.*

Proverbs 31:26: "She openeth her mouth with wisdom;
and in her tongue is the law of kindness."

Out of the Mouth of Babes

This account is not found in the Word of God. Matthew Henry says that it was written by Jewish writers who were fruitful in invention.

Mordecai was downcast and weary as he walked home from his work in the palace of the great King Ahasuerus. He had been sad and heavyhearted ever since he heard of Haman's awful plot to destroy the Jews.

Up ahead, Mordecai saw three bright-eyed Jewish children coming from school. He loved children. He always tried to take time to speak to them. In spite of the doom hanging over him, he paused to ask the children what they had learned that day.

"My lesson was Proverbs 3:25, 26. Be not afraid of sudden fear, neither of the desolation of the wicked, when it cometh. For the Lord shall be thy confidence, and shall keep thy foot from being taken," beamed the first child.

The second child told him his lesson was Isaiah 8:10. "Take counsel together, and it shall come to nought; speak the word, and it shall not stand: for God is with us."

"Isaiah 46:4 is what I learned today," announced the third child. "And even to your old age I am he; and even to hoar hairs will I carry you: I have made, and I will bear; even I will carry, and will deliver you."

The words of the children brought comfort and confidence to Mordecai. He desired that Esther might be told of his encounter with them. He longed for the by-gone days when he could freely talk with her. So many things had changed, yet God had not changed.

Mordecai knew his God would see him through these difficult days. God would provide and care for his people.

read and consider...

Where do we go to find encouragement?
Why is it important to take time to talk to children?

Read Psalm 8.
Proverbs 14:26: "In the fear of the LORD is strong confidence: and his children shall have a place of refuge."

Loaded With Faults

Two men came to visit my wife Susie and me. They came to tell us of our many faults. They told us the things they did not appreciate about us. Their gun was loaded.

While they were talking, I loaded my old double barrel. My mind raced as I filled my gun with an equal amount of things that I did not like about them.

When they had aired all their complaints, my retaliation was swift and true.

They were unhappy when they went home. My wife and I were unhappy too. We would have to have more meetings until we got our differences settled.

I realize now that I was in the wrong. I told my wife that when I am confronted again, I hope to be manly enough to shake hands and thank them.

Before God I will search myself. I will search for any nugget of truth in what is said. I will seek to improve and grow.

If only I had responded like my friend Joe. He was walking out to his car after services one evening. Matt followed him to his vehicle and gave him a real tongue lashing. He raked him up and down.

When Matt was done airing his complaints, the accused man humbly held out his hand. "Thank you, Brother," he said. "I also have many faults that you know nothing of; pray for me." Joe got in his car and was soon on his way home. As he was driving down the highway, suddenly a car blinked its lights and drove up close behind him.

"What a day," Joe sighed. "Am I to be robbed yet, too?"

Joe pulled over and was relieved to see Matt walk up. Matt said, "I want to apologize for my rash words to you tonight. I did not have the spirit of love. Pray for me that I would respond to criticism like you did."

read and consider...

If you don't like something about your brother, what should you do before you talk to him?

How was Joe able to respond so kindly to Matt?

What do you do when your parents reprimand you?

Read: Isaiah 53:7 and 1 Peter 2:23.

James 5:16: "Confess your faults one to another and pray one for another, that ye may be healed. The effectual fervent prayer of a righteous man availeth much."

Wise or Wagging

As a fire under control gives warmth and light,
So a tongue controlled by God gives warmth and
   blessing.

The school children were excitedly filing onto the bus
for the field trip. *Everyone seems happy but me*, Joseph
thought. *It seems like the boys are all against me. I wonder
if anyone likes me at all?* Joseph looked at the floor as he
walked to the back of the bus.

Just then, an older boy called out, "Hey, Joseph,
come sit with me."

Joseph's face broke into a glad smile. He felt so much
happier now. Someone actually was friendly to him.

Years later, Joseph was working on a construction
job. "Be careful, Joseph, don't get hurt; we need you,"
warned his boss.

Those words sang in Joseph's heart. *It certainly is more
fun and pleasant to work for some one who cares about
and appreciates me*, Joseph thought.

More years went by. Joseph grew up to be a fine,
dedicated young man. He was friendly and took an interest in others.

One day, he got a phone call that surprised him. "We
would like for you to be a dean at Calvary Bible School."

After much prayer and counsel from his parents,
Joseph went to Arkansas. Being a dean was a lot of work.
He taught Bible classes and worked with the students.

On a lovely sunny day, Joseph was sitting at his desk
by an open window, diligently studying for his class. Out-

side his window a group of students was talking. Joseph heard his name. They were actually discussing how Joseph taught. They didn't know he was listening. What Joseph heard was not encouraging to a teacher.

At the end of a three-week term at Bible school, a student handed Joseph a note. "The words he wrote were such an encouragement," Joseph later said. "He thanked me for my contribution to his life. He thanked me for the way I related to the boys on their level, and for how I played basketball with them."

"In spite of my poor memory, I still remember both of these incidents—even though they happened long ago." Joseph remarked. "I have learned that our words carry much weight. They have the power to influence for good or for ill."

No man can train his tongue; it takes a higher power. How much we need the help of God!

read and consider...

Do you take an interest in children who are younger than you are?

How do you talk about your teacher?

Read Proverbs 18:21 and Numbers 12:8.

Ephesians 4:29: "Let no corrupt communication proceed out of your mouth, but that which is good for the use of edifying, that it may minister grace unto the hearers."

A Thousand Tongues

Charles Wesley was a man so full of love and praise to God that he wrote 6,500 hymns! He had such a passion for the souls of men that he preached in churches, mining camps, and prisons from Scotland to Wales. He loved to sing Isaac Watt's hymn, "I'll Praise My Maker While I've Breath."

A Moravian leader, Peter Bohler, once told Charles, "Brother Wesley, the Lord has done so much for my life. Had I a thousand tongues, I would praise Christ Jesus with every one of them!"

Those words were a source of inspiration to Charles. He pondered them. On May 21, 1749, he wrote the hymn "O For a Thousand Tongues to Sing."

> Oh, for a thousand tongues to sing my great Redeemer's praise,
> The glories of my God and King, the triumphs of His grace.
> Hear Him ye deaf; His praise, ye dumb, your loosened tongues employ;
> Ye blind behold your Savior come, and leap ye lame for joy.
> Glory to God and praise and love, be ever, ever giv'n
> By saints below and saints above—the church in earth and heav'n.

That hymn has blessed many people, including Billy Bray, a man who was zealous for God in a life of faith and praise. He was born on June 1, 1794, in Truro, Cornwall, England. His early years were spent in mischief and drunkenness. God, in his great love and mercy, touched Billy's heart, and he became a changed man—a most effective witness for God.

Joyfulness of spirit was one of Billy Bray's outstanding characteristics. Of course, he had trials just as everyone does, but he said, "I have a heaven while going to heaven. Should not I praise God every step of the way?"

At a church meeting, Billy gave out a hymn and read the first line, "Oh for a thousand tongues to sing. . . ." He paused, "Just think of that! That is nine hundred and ninety-nine more tongues than I have! Many of you don't sing with the one tongue you have, and fuss when I try to use the one I have. If Wesley wished for nine hundred and ninety-nine more tongues, it would be a hard thing if I could not use my tongue in praise to my God!"

Billy liked to refer to himself as "The King's Son." He trusted his King implicitly for his and his family's every need. He invested nearly all his money in God's work.

Once a friend said to him, "Here is a coat and a waistcoat the Lord told me to give you. Try them on; don't know whether they will fit or not."

Billy confidently stated, "They will fit all right if the Lord told you to give them. He knows my size exactly. Fashion and I quarreled once, and we've never made up!"

Like his Master, Billy went about doing good as long as he was able. He visited the sick and needy. He preached, fasted, prayed and praised the Lord. His passion for the lost was a living fire in his breast. To the end, he praised the Lord. He was called to eternal glory when he was 74 years of age. His last breathe was spent in shouting "Glory!" Thus he entered that land of eternal splendor where ten thousand times ten thousand, and thousands of thousands of tongues praise their Maker forevermore.

read and consider...

What inspired Charles Wesley to write "Oh, For a Thousand Tongues to Sing"?

Mention a number of things Billy Bray loved to do.

Read: Revelation 5:9–14.

Psalm 150:6: "Let every thing that hath breath praise the LORD. Praise ye the LORD."

The Horse That Worked for God

"Glory, glory, bless the Lord!" shouted Billy Bray as he stood on the foundation stone of the chapel he was building for the Lord.

He preached his first sermon there on that stone. In Billy's neighborhood there were many wicked, ungodly people. There were few churches. Billy felt the Lord wanted him to build a chapel at Cross Lanes, near his house.

"If this new chapel stands for one hundred years, and one soul is converted every year, that will be a hundred souls; and one soul is worth more than all Cornwall," Billy declared. He was so excited about the prospect of future victories that he praised and blessed God even though he did not have enough funds to build a chapel! God provided the funds for that chapel just in time for each need.

Billy was overjoyed when he was given enough money for lumber, but he had no way of hauling the boards to the site of the Lord's house.

A kind neighbor said, "I have a horse and a cart, but my horse is so stubborn I cannot get her to haul a thing."

"I desperately need to get my lumber home," Billy stated. "Would you let me try your horse?"

"You can surely try my horse," said the man, "but you won't get her to pull a load, I warn you."

Billy took the neighbor's horse and cart and bravely set out to get the lumber. Everything went smoothly. How

Billy rejoiced and thanked the Lord when the lumber was unloaded at the chapel site.

"I never saw a better mare," Billy told the owner when he returned the horse. "Why, I did not use the whip once, not even on the steepest hill."

The neighbor was astonished. "How can it be?" he exclaimed. "You must be an authority with horses. Why, I never heard of such a thing! She certainly will not pull anything for me!"

"Well," said Billy in his own humble way, "that horse was not working for Billy Bray, or she would have been as mean as with anyone else. No, she was pulling this time for a very strong company: the Father, the Son, and the Holy Ghost, whom horses, as well as angels, men and devils, must obey. Yes, indeed, my Lord is an expert with horses!"

Resource: Anna Talbot McPherson, *Spiritual Secrets of Famous Christians,* Zondervan Publishing House, Grand Rapids, MI, 1964, pages 100-108.

read and consider...

Why did the horse willingly pull Billy's load?

Read: Psalm 71:14–16.
Psalm 72:18, 19: "Blessed be the LORD God, the God of Israel, who only doeth wondrous things. And blessed be his glorious name forever: and let the whole earth be filled with His glory; Amen, and Amen."

Provoking Brothers

Conflict among brothers is as old as the first pair of brothers, Cain and Abel.

There was not an actual line down the middle of the room that Sheldon and Brian shared. But it was understood that the room was divided. Half of the room was Sheldon's and the other half belonged to Brian.

Brian was a tease and could provoke Sheldon easily. Brian could just reach out and touch Sheldon's bed and Sheldon became upset about such a little thing.

One day the one who teased and the one who got mad went further than they meant to go. But that is often the case with anger, for anger clouds the mind and causes one to do what one did not actually want to.

"Get your hand off my bed, Brian," Sheldon muttered darkly. "You'd better quit that, or I'm going to do something."

Brian grinned and kept teasing. Again and again, he reached out and touched his brother's bed.

Sheldon grabbed a belt. Wildly he struck at his brother's hand. The belt buckle hit the offending finger with a forceful crack. Brian's fingernail popped off, and Brian yelled in pain.

Their parents had a good talk with them that evening. "You will always be brothers," Dad said. "The sooner you both learn to love each other and be peacemakers, the happier our home will be. You will be happier, too."

The boys looked at each other sheepishly. They both apologized for having gone too far. That night there was peace in their room.

Will you choose to love your brother? Or will you destroy him as Cain destroyed Abel?

read and consider...

How will you show love to your brother today?
What should you do when your brother is unkind?

Read: Proverbs 16:32 and 1 John 4:20.
Proverbs 14:17: "He that is soon angry dealeth foolishly."

Who Controls Your Tongue?

Aden Troyer was the evangelist at tent meetings far from his home in Ohio. One evening at the meetings, a young man came up to him and said, "Brother Aden, how much did you fast for these tent meetings?"

Self reared his ugly head and whispered to Aden, "That young man is cocky; ask him, 'How much did *you* fast? How much did you put in the offering plate on Sunday?'"

By the grace of God, Brother Aden rose to the challenge and responded, "Not enough."

Before you speak, think. Let your words pass this test:

- T — Is it true?
- H — Will it help?
- I — Will it inspire?
- N — Is it necessary?
- K — Is it kind?

Do not be like the two ladies who were sharing a juicy tidbit about a neighbor over the backyard fence.

"Tell me more," said the one.

The other lady replied, "I can't. I already told you more than what I heard.

"My talent is to speak my mind," a woman once told John Wesley. He told her, "That is one talent God would not mind you burying."

read and consider...

Do you try to say nice things about others each day?
Ask God to help you develop a tongue that is kind.

Read Psalm 19:14 and Ephesians 4:29.
Psalm 141:3: "Set a watch, O Lord, before my mouth; keep the door of my lips."

CHAPTER 9

Work and Ordinary Days

Wonderful Work

My legs take me where I want to go
My hands knead the soft bread dough,
My fingers work, all ten of them,
To comb my hair, or mend a hem,
Lord, help me my duties never to shirk,
I am so thankful I can work!

—Mary Ellen Beachy

Be Diligent

"Marcellus," I called to my small son from the kitchen where I was peeling potatoes for supper. "Marcellus, run and do your chores before we eat."

Marcellus did not want to gather the eggs or feed the dog. But he knew he must obey. So, with a little pail in his hand and a frown on his face, he slowly, very slowly, shuffled out to the chicken house.

In just a few minutes, I was surprised to see him running back to the house at top speed. His face was all wreathed in smiles. "Mom, Mom," he hollered, "Mom, I heard a little peeping noise in the corner of the chicken house. I saw a broken eggshell, and then I saw a tiny little bantam chick was snuggled under the mother hen. It's so cute. Whoopie!" Off he raced to the chicken house again with his brothers and sisters in hot pursuit.

Boys and chores, what a winning combination! And it is better yet when boys learn to do their work without complaining.

read and consider...

It is such a blessing to like to work!
What are some of your jobs?

Read: Luke 16:10-12.
Ecclesiastes 9:10: "Whatsoever thy hand findeth to do, do it
    with thy might."

Be Honest

Every time Tommy went to the feed mill, he checked his pockets to see if he had a nickel. You see, Tommy liked the little packs of peanuts that came out of the machine when he put a nickel in the slot and turned the knob.

One day when Tommy was searching for a nickel, he pulled a washer out of his pocket. He looked at it and thought, *This looks like it is the same size as a nickel. I wonder. . . .* He put the washer in the slot, turned the knob, and amazingly out slid a delicious pack of his favorite peanuts! Wow, that was cheap!

Now when Tommy went to the feed mill, he made sure a washer was in his pocket!

A few years later, Tommy asked the Lord Jesus to live in his heart. He asked God to forgive all the wrongs he had ever done. Suddenly in his mind he saw those washers and the many little packs of peanuts. The next day, he went back to the feed mill, told the manager what he had done, and paid what he figured all those peanuts had cost.

A preacher once shared this story:

"Over the hills from our house lives a friend who buys vitamins from us. He is a big Dutchman with broad shoulders, big arms, and a big smile. One day he brought an invoice back to our house. He put his arm around my shoulder, and smiling from ear to ear, he said, "You didn't charge us enough for this one item. We try to not cheat anyone. We want to go to heaven. We can't stumble through life any old way and expect to get there!"

And then there was Richard Mumaw. When he became a Christian, he had much restitution to make. The Lord brought to his mind that he had stolen a jack from a large department store years before. He went back to that town and after much searching, he found the store. He asked for the manager and was sent to see a lady. He told her he had stolen a jack years ago which was worth $9.97. The lady was quite amazed that someone who had gotten away with stealing would ever return to make things right!

read and consider...

Why did Tommy at first think it was smart to get peanuts with a washer?

Why is it so important for God's children to be honest?

Read: Ephesians 4:29.

Romans 13:13: "Let us walk honestly, as in the day."

How to Be Big

At times we long to do something BIG for Jesus! It would seem like a BIG thing to be a missionary, a preacher, a nurse, or a teacher.

Always remember, it is a BIG thing to be faithful at home, doing whatever God has given you to do!

In God's eyes, faithfulness is what counts: faithfulness in doing whatever duty God sends your way—especially work that needs to be done for your family in your home. No one may seem to see or appreciate what you do, but God will see your faithfulness.

Jenny Evelyn Hussey, a devout Quaker, felt as though she spent much of her life hidden away in the country. She longed for opportunities to tell people how much she loved Jesus, but her days were filled with taking care of her helpless invalid sister. Though she longed to do more, she did not complain and grow bitter. Cheerful coura-geousness marked her days. She accepted caring for her sister as "from the Lord."

She "practiced the presence of Jesus" as she went about each day's duties. Truly, His sweet presence gave her the strength she needed to cheerfully do ordinary and thankless tasks.

Later in life, Jenny was severely tried with deformative arthritis. Out of that hardship and suffering, God gave her a song that placed her name among the gospel hymn writers. Jenny Evelyn Hussey is credited with writing 150 hymns.

Through her trials, Jenny said, "Please, Lord, make me willing to bear my cross daily without complaining, because you bore yours for me."[1] She wrote the lovely words of "Lead Me to Calvary," blessing the world with a song because she had learned the lessons of submission by saying "yes" to God. She did something big for Jesus by being faithful.

May I be willing Lord to bear,
Daily my cross for Thee,
Even thy cup of grief to share,
Thou hast borne all for me.

Resource: Alfred Smith, *Al Smiths Treasuries of Hymn Histories*, Heritage Music Distributors, Montrose, Pennsylvania, 1981.

read and consider...

How can we do difficult duties cheerfully?
What may be some reasons God's children are sick at times?

Read Hebrews 12:1-3.
Romans 8:18, 37: "For I reckon that the sufferings of this present time are not worthy to be compared with the glory which shall be revealed in us. . . . Nay, in all these things we are more than conquerors through him that loved us."

Seven Sheep

Mission work is hard work! It often costs thousands of miles of travel and leaving behind dear parents, relatives, and friends. Is it worth the cost?

Consider this story and what the destiny of these dear souls would have been if no one had pointed them to Jesus.

Randy Lapp, a missionary to Kenya, said, "Mission work is God's work. When things go well, we give Him the glory. When things are difficult, we bring our needs and cares to Him!

"I will tell you of one *mzee* (old man) who is a member of the church in Engashura," Randy said. "His name is Gichohi Thumbi. This man is in his upper seventies. He is willing to work hard and never begs for assistance, though he is physically small, quite old, and has weak eyes. The missionaries learned to know him through his egg-peddling business. He would buy eggs and walk long distances to deliver them to his customers."

Randy is challenged many times by the way Gichohi continues to work in spite of his age. He also has a milk cow, a heifer, and a calf that he is raising, plus a one-acre garden that he and his wife tend.

At one time, Gichohi had seven sheep. These sheep were special. They were his life savings, his retirement plan. But alas, one day a leopard escaped from a game park. That hungry leopard killed all seven of the old man's sheep.

"Gichohi attends church very faithfully. The very next Sunday after his sheep were killed, he stood to give a testimony in church. He said emphatically that in spite of his troubles, he is not defeated and will continue on with the Lord! Amen!

"He loves church and leans forward with his head cocked so he can catch everything that is said."

Randy says that whenever he feels discouraged with church difficulties and needs encouragement, he can find it at Gichohi's house. Gichohi cannot read. But he has memorized many Bible stories, which he happily tells to anyone who will listen. His favorite story is about the woman who was sick for twelve years and was healed when she touched the hem of Jesus' garment.

One day Gichohi told Randy that he and his wife's marriage was arranged by their parents when they were both children. His father began to pay the dowry when Gichohi was but a lad. When they were old enough to marry, everything was in order.

"Did your parents make a good choice for you?" Randy asked.

Gichohi turned to look at his wife and with a wide smile on his face, he stated, "I love her!" What a blessing!

read and consider...

What a joy it is when people enjoy work. Have you learned to do your duties cheerfully?

How can we learn to trust God through difficult losses?

Sing the song, "Lord, Prepare Me to Be a Missionary."

Read: Acts 1:8 and Acts 4:12, 13.

Isaiah 6:8: "And I heard the voice of the LORD saying, Whom shall I send, and who will go for us? Then said I, Here am I; send me."

A Comfort for Many

One person with a heart full of love for God can make a difference! Simon Smoker is an 84-year-old widower. He is busy serving the Lord. In 11 years time, Simon has sewn a total of 4,127 comforters to be distributed to needy people around the world.

In 1976, Simon's wife Irene became ill with Alzheimer disease. She needed considerable care for many years. Simon chose to lovingly care for her rather than putting her into a nursing home.

The 1980s were difficult years for Simon. Many times he was unable to attend church services, but one Sunday in 1985 a friend said, "I will stay with Irene today so you can go to church."

At the services that day, he picked up a brochure explaining the need for blankets in Africa. Simon thought he could help with that project of reaching out to needy people. He felt the Lord was asking him to do what he could, so he began to sew comforters. He often worked on these blankets late into the night while he cared for his wife.

God called Irene home in 1990. Simon was lonely and decided to do some traveling. During this time his work on comforters slowed down. But in 1991, he made 100 comforters and since then, the amount has been increasing. Some years Simon has sewn over 700 comforters! Most of these he gave to Christian Aid Ministries. Making comforters gives Simon a purpose, it keeps him in shape, and helps to pass the time in a meaningful way. His work blesses the lives of many who are poor and cold.

One man's labor of love is truly a comfort to many.

Christian Aid Ministries newsletter, December, 1996
Used by permission.

read and consider...

If you don't know what to do, why not pray, "Lord, what will you have me to do today?"

Read: 2 Corinthians 9:6–8.

Matthew 25:40: "And the King shall answer and say unto them, "Verily I say unto you, Inasmuch as ye have done it unto one of the least of these my brethren, ye have done it unto me."

A Gift You'd Never Trade

Here is a riddle for you:

What highly precious gift did God give each of us which we use every day?

They are fascinating and useful.

We use them nearly all the time, unless we are resting or sleeping.

The five things attached to them are extremely helpful.

Without our _____ we would be quite crippled.

With our _____ we can help or hurt others.

By now, you have surely guessed that this wonderful gift is your hands.

One small boy once guessed the answer was the mouth, but I am so grateful we have only *one* mouth!

With gratitude I think of my parents' toil-worn hands. Their hands met my needs countless times when I was a baby and all through my years at home. Today, their hands continue to love and bless me.

The hands of so many people have brightened my days. Whenever we go back to my home community, my Uncle Amos and Aunt Lydia welcome us with warm and caring handshakes. Their hands are always ready to help with any work that needs to be done.

I am so thankful for my husband's strong, loving hands which provide so well for me. I never fear his big hands; what a blessing they are!

There is much potential in my children's hands. It is amazing what their hands can do: pick berries, sweep the floor, bake bread, hold the kitties, sew, and much more.

I love the warm hugs they give me. (Imagine a hug without hands!)

My little boys love to use their hands to pick flowers. They'll run to me, each holding a little bouquet behind their backs, their faces beaming with smiles as they ask, "Which hand, Mama?"

Once our family spent the night at a cabin without electricity. "Mom, I need a hand," my little son's voice woke me from sweet slumber. I reached out to grasp his hand in the darkness. My hand provided all the comfort he craved.

I admire the beauty of dainty, feminine hands. I remember saying to my mother years ago, "My hands are not pretty." She wisely responded, "Be thankful they are strong." Since then, I have learned the truth of the old saying, "The most beautiful hands are those which are found ready to bless and help their fellowmen."

I find it interesting that the word *hand* is found in Scripture over 1,500 times! No other hands have blessed and helped mankind like the nail-pierced hands of our Savior.

Jesus' hands lovingly helped people in need. His tender touch healed thousands. At the end of a life of giving, He stretched out His hands to embrace all of humanity in his death.

read and consider...

How can you use your hands to bless your family and others?
What is special about the hands of Jesus?
As I look at my own hands I like to pray: "Lord, in what way can my hands bless others today?"

Read: Psalm 31:5 and John 10:29.
Psalm 95:7: "He is our God; we are the people of his pasture, and the sheep of his hand."

Nine Hundred Men

Where are the young men who are wholly given to the cause of Christ? Where are the parents who are willing to raise and train their children for the work of God?

One time, a discouraged prison chaplain called Nelson Coblentz. "We have nine hundred men in this prison," the chaplain said. "Nine hundred men who are very uncooperative and rebellious. Half of our prison staff has resigned because they cannot handle these men. What I need, Nelson, is five or six young Christian men who are willing to be role models to these men, to socialize with them and have recreation with them. These men desperately need someone to care about them and love them."

Nelson wished he could say, "Yes, here are men to meet the need." But he did not know of five or six young men who would be willing to work full time in the "white and ready-for-harvest" prison field. Could he find even one or two?

Where are the young men who are wholly given to the cause of Christ? Where are the parents who are willing to raise and train their children for the work of God? God has a work and a plan for each boy and girl, each man and woman. God can use one dedicated life to touch thousands of people.

That's what Fannie Crosby did, even though she was blind. Her mother and grandmother had a vision for helping Fannie memorize many Scripture passages. Thus, her life was touched for God at a very early age. One afternoon when Fannie was eight or nine years old, she went out into the fields. She dedicated her life to God and asked Him to use her for some good, pure, and noble purpose. When she came home, she jotted down her first beautiful lines of poetry.

> Oh what a happy soul I am, although I cannot see;
> I am resolved that in this world contented I will be.
> How many blessings I enjoy that other people don't;
> To weep and sigh because I am blind, I cannot and I
> won't.

Fannie wrote between seven and eight thousand poems and hymns in her lifetime. How many hearts has she touched for God through her gift of poetry? Nine hundred men? Nine thousand men? Nine hundred thousand men?

read and consider...

What can you do now to prepare to be a worker for God?
What helped inspire Fannie Crosby to write so many songs?
Many of the songs you sing today were written by Fannie Crosby. Watch for her songs in your songbooks.

Read: Colossians 3:2 and John 4:35.
Matthew 6:33: "But seek ye first the kingdom of God, and his righteousness; and all these things shall be added unto you."

The Little Nurse

Clara knelt in the straw beside the family pet. Large tears rolled down her cheeks as she looked at the mangled and crushed paw of Patch, their big hunting dog. The whole family was very fond of him. Clara said that Patch even came to say good morning to her each day. Now he had been run over by a farm wagon.

"Don't even touch that paw if he growls," warned Clara's big brother David.

In her sweet, gentle voice Clara began softly crooning to Patch. "I'll take care of you, you poor, poor Patch," she murmured.

Very, very gently she washed the dog's paw, and carefully put salve on it. When she was done, Patch gratefully licked her hand. Every day she fed him and put on a clean bandage. Before long, he was well and strong again.

The neighbor children brought their sick pets to Clara. Clara loved them all—puppies, kittens, and even a sick ground hog. Most of them got well and thrived under Clara's love and care.

When Clara's brother David fell from the rafters at a barn raising, she spent hours each day cheerfully caring for him. Soon she was affectionately known as the "Little Nurse."

Later, Clara could well have been called the "Little Teacher," for she was only 15 on her first day as a schoolteacher.

Clara was worried about some of the older boys who had a reputation for being bullies. No wonder she was worried, for at recess one day she heard a commotion on the playground and rushed to the window.

To her dismay, she saw the big boys throwing the little boys into the mud and then rolling them in it. She absolutely could not stand to see the strong hurt the weak.

She marched to the door and blew a loud blast with her brother's hunting whistle. The surprised bullies stopped in their tracks. Instead of scolding them, she asked them to fetch a heavy keg of cider from her buggy. All the children gathered around and enjoyed the unexpected treat.

Clara organized recess so that there was no time to run wildly over the playground. She taught the older ones a new ball game that required strength, skill, and speed. She earned the boys' respect and admiration. After two months of school, the older boys were no longer mean bullies. There were only boys, anxious to please Clara and happy to learn.

She taught the children the importance of looking respectable by wearing clean clothes and having clean hands and faces. How happy she was when the bullies no longer came to school dirty and disheveled.

In later years, Clara Barton was a nurse. She founded the American Red Cross. She took charge of relief work in the flood of Johnstown, Pennsylvania, in 1889. She lived an unselfish life, helping anyone who was in need.

How did Clara win the respect of her students?

What are some things she did to help others?

Make it a daily goal to do something to help others, for Jesus
sake. It will lead you to the pathway of joy and happiness.

Read: Ephesians 5:1, 2.

Titus 3:8: "This is a faithful saying, and these things I will that
thou affirm constantly, that they which have believed in
God might be careful to maintain good works. These things
are good and profitable to men."

Diamond in the Rough

Eight-year-old Annie was a sad, lonely little girl. And no wonder, for her mother had just died. The oldest of five children, Annie tried to keep house for her father while her siblings went to live with relatives. But, sadly, her father was often drunk and difficult, and they were very poor.

Her parents had fled Ireland during the Great Famine in the 1840s. They had come to the New World in search of a better life.

Annie could not see well. Her father took her to a doctor who said she had an eye disease called trachoma which would cause her eyes to always be inflamed.

She was not the most pleasant child. She often had outbursts of temper. Her father tired of her, and Annie went to join her five-year-old brother Jimmie at their aunt and uncle's home. Jimmie had been born with tuberculosis and walked with a crutch. Their father promised to help support his children, but he did not keep his word. Because of her poor eyesight, Annie could not go to school. The motherless children were considered a burden and, at last, were sent away to a poorhouse (a place where orphans and old folks were kept).

Annie sent up a loud wail when she and Jimmie were to be separated. Thankfully, the staff had pity on Annie and allowed her and Jimmie to stay together. Annie would not let her frail brother out of her sight. But Jimmie became ill and died a few months later. Poor Annie felt so lost and alone.

After Annie had lived for years in the dreary poorhouse, a man who was sent to investigate the conditions there took an interest in her. He arranged for her to join the Perkins Institute for the blind. A ray of hope and sunshine shone into Annie's life.

Talking back to her teachers, throwing tantrums, and telling lies got Annie into trouble. The loving teachers took her firmly in hand, and she responded to their love and discipline. Annie became a bright, attractive student.

Annie was sent to doctors for eye surgeries. Finally, her eyes were so much improved that she could read anything. She was overjoyed!

Twenty-year-old Annie graduated at the top of her class at Perkins. And one day, Perkins Institute was contacted by Captain Keller. He was desperately searching for a companion and teacher for his blind and deaf daughter Helen.

So Annie, who had been troubled about what she would do after graduation, went to join the Keller family. Little did she know that this new job would last for the rest of her life. She would find fulfillment and even become famous!

Do you ever feel that you have no talents, that your family is not popular, or that you are poor or not very pretty? Take heart. Like Annie Sullivan, you are a diamond in the rough.

God truly does care about you. He has a plan and a purpose for your life. Give yourself to Him, and He will make something beautiful and good.

(to be continued)

What were some of the very difficult things in Annie's life?

Is anyone beyond help?

Does anyone need your love and encouragement?

Read: Isaiah 61:1–3 and Luke 4:18, 19.

Matthew 20:27, 28: "And whosoever will be chief among you, let him be your servant: even as the Son of man came not to be ministered unto, but to minister, and to give his life a ransom for many."

Rescued From the Dark and Dismal

Annie watched in amazement and dismay as the untidy little girl walked around the breakfast table sniffing the food. She grabbed whatever she pleased from other's plates and no one stopped her! After all, the child was blind and deaf!

When seven-year-old Helen tried to grab food from Annie's plate, Annie calmly moved her plate. This aggravated the child, and she pinched Annie. Annie slapped her. Helen threw a tantrum. She fell to the kitchen floor kicking and trying to pull Annie's chair away. Helen was determined to have her own way. But she had met her match.

Annie knew Helen must learn two very important things in life: love and obedience. Only then could she be happy and live a useful life.

Could Annie find the jewel of a child buried under the resistant wild creature?

She was ready to do battle. Day by day, she patiently labored with little Helen. To teach her to do very simple things, Annie had to use force. Helen wanted to eat with her hands. Annie insistently gave her a spoon. Her family became upset, particularly her father who did not like to see his daughter cry.

One time Helen became so angry that her hand flew up and knocked out one of Annie's front teeth.

Annie spelled words into Helen's hand over and over. Light finally dawned in her mind. She learned to associate words with things. Eventually, she learned to spell, write, and even to talk.

One night after weeks of hard work, Helen stole into Annie's arms and kissed her for the first time. Annie was so overjoyed she thought her heart would burst!

Little by little, Helen responded to Annie's firm, quiet love. The wild lass was taught, trained, and became a joyful child.

Helen's parents were so thankful for the big change in their daughter. Her mother said, "I thank God every day in my life for sending you to us."

In later years, Helen and Annie did much to help the plight of the deaf and the blind: the people who stared into the dark with nothing but the dark staring back. They gave many speeches, a living testimony that the blind and the deaf, many who were totally idle, could be trained to become skilled workers and a benefit and blessing to society.

Helen and Annie were best of friends. Helen loved and appreciated her teacher who had rescued her from her silent black night. Helen said, "She unlocked the gates of my being, and I stretched out my hands in the quest of life."

Through Annie's patient work, Helen became famous. Her teacher was content to be in the background, quiet and truly great.

Resources: Bernice Seldon, *The Story of Annie Sullivan, Helen Keller's Teacher*, Parachute Press, 1987, page 94

What two things did Helen need to learn?
How did Annie help her?

Read: Proverbs 29:15 and Proverbs 23:25.
Proverbs 29:17: "Correct thy son, and he shall give thee rest;
    yea, he shall give delight unto thy soul."

Before You Are Fourteen

There are several arts which every girl can learn before she is 14 years old. Look at them, and see if you don't think they are within your reach.

1. Shut the door and shut it softly.
2. Keep your room in tasteful order.
3. Have a time set for rising in the morning and keep it.
4. Learn to make bread as well as cake.
5. Never let a button stay off twenty-four hours.
6. Always know where your things are.
7. Never let a day pass without doing something to make somebody comfortable and happy.
8. Never go with your shoes unfastened.
9. Speak clearly enough for everyone to understand.
10. Never fidget or hum to disturb others.

Resource: *Words of Cheer*, Herald Press, Scottdale, Pennsylvania, October 1944.

Bad Habits

Bad little habits can grow by degrees
Until they become dangerous as roaring seas.
Bad little habits do grow sometimes,
Until they do lead to terrible crimes.
The boy or the girl who would happy be
From bad little habits must ever keep free.
—Dorothy C. Retsloff

10
chapter ten

Influence

Vision

I see God in the morning light,
I see Him in the trees,
I see Him in the stars of night
And in small humming bees.

I see Him in the garden flowers,
I see Him in the sea,
And pray that everyone I meet
Will see His love in me.

— Author Unknown

Showers of Blessing

We imagine this song being sung when a gentle rain is falling over a prosperous, peaceful land in the green springtime.

Amazingly, this song came to the mind of a man in a prison in Vietnam during a thunderstorm when torrents of rain flooded the jungles and the dismal prison. The words uplifted and blessed his soul in a time of great need.

Imagine being a prisoner of war in Vietnam for seven long, lonely years. Howard Rutledge was a prisoner. His food was little more than a bowl of pig fat. He was often cold, lonely, and cruelly treated. Some men in such a terrible place give up. How then did Howard survive? How did he keep his sanity?

Prison showed Howard the emptiness of life without God. He knew, there in that horrible prison, that he needed God. He could not have what he longed for: a Bible, a songbook, or a preacher. He tried to remember all the wonderful words of life he had been taught long ago, when as a child he went to Sunday school in Tulsa, Oklahoma. He was delighted that he could recall three dozen choruses and hymns from his Sunday school days.

Each day in prison Howard tried to remember another verse or song. One night he was going over hymn tunes in his mind. A tropical storm blew in. The thunder boomed and the rain fell in torrents. A bolt of lightning knocked out the lights. The prison was plunged into blackness. Suddenly, a song he had entirely forgotten flooded his mind.

There shall be showers of blessing!
Oh that today they might fall,
Now as to God we're confessing,
Now as on Jesus we call.

Howard's spirit was not crushed in his forsaken cell. God's words, God's songs were his bread, his joy, and life to his innermost soul, enabling him to have victory over the enemy and the power of death around him.

read and consider...

Thank God if you have the opportunity to go to Sunday school!
Thank God for the many songs you sing.
Why is it such a good thing to have God's Word hidden in your heart?
When all else is taken from you, is God enough?

Read: 2 Timothy 3:15–17.
Psalm 19:7: "The law of the LORD is perfect, converting the soul: the testimony of the LORD is sure, making wise the simple."

Water the Seed

Have your parents ever needed to remind you of the verse, "Be ye kind one to another," or the verse, "Blessed are the peacemakers for they shall be called the children of God?" I hope that when you are tempted to fuss and fight with your brothers and sisters, you will think of those verses and choose to be a peacemaker. I am trying to teach my children kindness and other character traits that please the Lord. It is something I need to work on daily, and not give up.

One autumn day I heard one of my little boys holler. The boys had been raking leaves. I looked out the door and saw one lad running with his rake held high. I sighed, "How can it be that they even chase each other with a rake?" Upon investigation, I found that Matthias had wanted to get the dog off the porch and the dog snapped at him. Marcellus was coming with the rake to protect his brother. They did care for each other after all!

Another day, Micah was outside crying. I saw him sitting on the basketball court while his big brother was trying to comfort him. Another brother rushed in for a band-aid. Micah had stepped on a nail, and his brothers were being kind and caring!

I need to express appreciation to my children when they do kind deeds. That helps to water the seed of kindness. At other times I may ask, "Was that kind? Is that what Jesus would want you to do?"

I need the help of the Lord to respond with kind firmness when my children are unkind. I want to model kindness to my family. When I err, may I be kind enough to apologize. I want to be diligent each day to sow the seeds of kindness in the lives of my children, then water those seeds by kindness and prayer.

God, help my children grow up to become compassionate and caring individuals.

read and consider...

What do you do when someone is unkind?
How can you show kindness in your family?

Read 2 Peter 1:5–7.
Romans 12:10: "Be kindly affectioned one to another with brotherly love; in honour preferring one another."

There Is a God!

One day a teacher in an East German school told his class to say, "There is no God."

In his class was an eight-year-old girl from a Christian home. This little girl believed in God. Her parents prayed to Him. She knew God heard and answered their prayers. This was proof to her that there is a God. She refused to obey her teacher.

Try as he might, the teacher could not make her deny God. Finally he commanded her to go home and write, "There is no God" fifty times and bring it to school the next day.

That evening the girl told her mother what had happened. The mother did not know what to say for she was afraid of the Communists. That night the girl sat down and very courageously wrote, *"Es gibt noch ein Gott"* (There is a God).

The teacher's face flushed purple with rage when he read the words she had written. He commanded her to go home and write, "There is no God" five hundred times, "or else." The girl knew very well that "or else" meant death.

That evening she told her father what had happened at school. He looked at her with a smile of approval and with a calmness equal to hers, he said, "Tomorrow we shall both talk to the superintendent of the school. Let us trust God with the matter."

That night the small girl peacefully slept. She believed in God. She knew He would take care of her. The next morning the family knelt in prayer, asking God for His blessing and protection on their day.

They met with the superintendent about the trouble they were in. The man smiled and said, "Little girl, your teacher was killed in a motorcycle accident yesterday. The matter is finished."

My mother, a lover of good literature, sent me a clipping of this story. It was found in a church bulletin.

read and consider...

If others laugh or mock, do you have courage to stand for the right?

Why did the little girl believe there is a God?

Read: 2 Timothy 1:12–14.

Romans 1:16: "For I am not ashamed of the gospel of Christ: for it is the power of God unto salvation to every one that believeth; to the Jew first, and also to the Greek."

They Taught Me How to Worship

Everybody needs something worthwhile to do, a work that makes them useful to mankind, and a ministry that pleases God. Ask God what He wants you to do.

In Haiti, the youth need something better to do than just walking around town in the evening. They need a purpose in life. They need God. Christian Aid Ministries Teaching Program is a light in Haiti's darkness.

In Tetian, CAM started a three-week Bible seminar for young men. "We want to bring men to our mission compound and teach them from the Bible. We pray they will then go home and teach their families and their villages what they have learned. Our long-range goal is that some of these students will later return and teach their fellow Haitians these classes," relates Delbert Schrock, who currently teaches at this Bible school.

"Our very first seminar was attended by nine men. Three were assistant pastors, two were school directors, one was a teacher, and three were active laymen. These men came from rural mountain communities," says Delbert. "Imagine the interesting time I had teaching them how to use a shower and a toilet! We take showers and indoor bathrooms for granted, but they did not even know how to use them. They did not know what the bunk beds were for. I explained that to them too."

Delbert says, "I learned so much from them. They taught me how to worship God. They were so willing and eager to hear God's Word, I felt as if I were learning more than my students.

"Our seminar started with a devotional at 8:30 in the morning. We had classes from 9:00 to 3:00. For six hours I was teaching through an interpreter, my feet got tired standing on the hard cement floor. I was weary from the heat, too, but my students said, 'Teacher, we need to start earlier. 8:30 is too late.'

"They had such a hunger for the Word of God. It was no problem for them to study long hours in 100° to 105° temperatures. At their request, we started earlier. It was a wonderful experience."

Bible study books are rare in Haiti. At the end of the three weeks of classes, each man was given a Creole Bible Concordance. The men were grateful and excited that they now had a tool to help them find verses for themselves.

Story taken from Christian Aid Ministries Open House, 2004
Used by permission.

read and consider...

Pray for the Bible school in Haiti.
Do you know how to use a Bible concordance?

Read: Matthew 5:6 and Isaiah 55:1.
Jeremiah 15:16: "Thy words were found, and I did eat them; and thy word was unto me the joy and rejoicing of mine heart: for I am called by thy name, O LORD God of hosts."

Ten Thousand School Children

Many children in poverty-stricken Haiti cannot go to school. Their parents may be too poor, or there might be no school near enough to attend.

Yet many Haitians long for an education. Some are determined enough to go to school that they are willing to walk six miles—six miles one way.

If you could peek into schools in Haiti, you would see some very interesting and unique sights. Here comes Joseph, running to school carrying a piece of firewood. He hands it to the cook who is fanning a glowing fire on the ground. She opens a large bag of rice and pours it into the big black pot of boiling water and beans which hangs over her outdoor fire.

At lunchtime, Joseph and his friends come running to the big kettle, bringing the spoons and plates they brought from home. They are so hungry, and this will be their biggest meal for the day.

Oh dear, here comes a shy little boy who has no spoon. He squeezes in beside his friend. Will he just eat with his fingers? Ah, what a lovely sight. The two little boys share the spoon, each taking turns to scoop up a bite.

Many of the schools are simple shelters with a dirt floor. Some schools do not have desks. The children are happy anyhow, and they sit cross-legged on the floor holding their book and their tablet. Does the chalkboard up front look strange to you? It is just plywood painted green.

Christian Aid Ministries supports 50 schools in Haiti. They provide the students with books, tablets, pencils, and food. They also provide payment for the teachers. This is possible because Christians care to share, contributing to CAM's sponsorship program which supports ten thousand school children in Haiti. Christian Aid Ministries also provides teacher training retreats to equip the teachers to teach effectively.

A Haitian teacher said, "Please pray for me that God would give me more patience and love as I teach. My students may become tomorrow's Sunday school teachers, pastors, and preachers."

Derived from Christian Aid Ministries newsletter, August 25, 2003.
Used by permission.

read and consider...

You have so much, are you thankful?
What can you do to help the poor in Haiti?

Read 1 John 3:17, 18.
Luke 6:38: "Give, and it shall be given unto you; good measure, pressed down, and shaken together, and running over, shall men give into your bosom. For with the same measure that ye mete withal it shall be measured to you again."

From King to Cow

Nebuchadnezzar was a powerful king in the ancient world. He ruled over a vast empire and was famous for brilliant military exploits and for developing the great city of Babylon. During his 45 year reign, he never wearied of building and beautifying the palaces and temples of his city. He wanted his city to be the most notable in the world.

The walls of this wonder city were 60 miles around, 300 feet high, and 80 feet thick. The walls extended 35 feet below the ground. There were 250 towers on the walls and guard rooms for soldiers. Who could ever conquer such a city?

Nebuchadnezzar designed fabulous hanging gardens for one of his wives, a Median princess who was homesick for the mountains of her fatherland. These gardens were one of the seven wonders of the world.

His palace was one of the most magnificent buildings ever erected on earth. It was gorgeously decorated. The banquet hall and throne room was 56 feet wide and 168 feet long. The south walls of the throne room were 20 feet thick.

One night, as the king strolled on the roof of his royal residence and looked out over the city, he was puffed up with a great feeling of success and pride in what he had planned and accomplished. He said, "Is not this the great Babylon that I have built by my own mighty power and for the honor of my majesty?"

Proverbs 29:23 says that a man's pride shall bring him low. God hates pride. It is an abomination to him. And so, God sent Nebuchadnezzar to "Grass College." The king was driven away from people and his palace. He lived with the wild animals, ate grass with the cattle, and was drenched with heaven's dew.

How did he look? Was he really a cow? Whatever he was, it was some strange creature. Scripture records that his hair grew as long as eagle's feathers, his nails were like birds' claws. His heart was changed from a man's, and a beast's heart was given him. Thus he lived for seven years.

At the end of seven years, God restored Nebuchadnezzar's sanity. Then the king looked up to heaven and praised and worshipped the most high God. He said, "God's kingdom is forevermore. God does what He pleases. Every act of God is right. He takes those who walk proudly and pushes them in the dust. Now I will honor and glorify the God of heaven."

What about you and me? Do we praise God for the abilities and talents he has given us? If you are an excellent scholar, a powerful ball player, can bake delicious bread, or your garden and flower beds grow well, then stop and thank God for what He has given you. All you have received comes from God. Praise Him!

Today all the magnificence of Babylon lies in dust and ruins. Set your affections on God and that which lasts forever.

read and consider...

Thoughts to ponder: Pride makes us say things we should not and keeps us from saying what we should. Pride is thinking of self and not of others.

Read: Daniel 4 and Proverbs 29:23.

James 4:6: "God resisteth the proud, but giveth grace unto the humble."

Bathtub Blessings

My six-year-old son was enjoying his warm bath when he popped up with a question, "Mom, do you want to be on the narrow way or the broad way?"

"Well, the narrow way, honey, what about you?"

"The narrow way, too, Mom. We learned a song about that in school. Shall I sing it for you?"

In his sweet boyish voice, Marcellus sang for me:

> There are two ways built for little feet,
> That's the Bible story,
> The broad way is with danger filled,
> The straight way leads to glory.
> Which way are you traveling?
> Which way are you traveling,
> Which way are you traveling,
> The broad or narrow way?
> Oh how sweet to know that day by day,
> Jesus walks beside me,
> With my hand in his I cannot stray,
> And safely He will guide me.

"Mom," Marcellus continued, "my teacher told us a story about a man named Christian who was on the narrow way."

That conversation and song blessed me abundantly. It made me so thankful for a Christian school and for godly teachers.

Why is it a good thing for little children to learn godly songs?

What do your parents do to encourage you to be on the narrow
way?

Read: Matthew 7:13, 14.

John 14:5, 6: "Thomas saith unto Him, Lord, we know not
whither thou goest; and how can we know the way? Jesus
saith unto him, I am the way, the truth, and the life: no man
cometh unto the Father but by me."

Who Will Teach Our Children?

"How is Wendell doing with his school work?" Lester asked the teacher at the parent teacher's fellowship.

"Wendell? Ah yes, Wendell. Ah, I believe he is doing all right, Mr. Miller. There are 70 first graders you know, but yes, yes, your son does fine."

"Les," Betty said on their way home from PTF, "I think Wendell's teacher didn't really know which child was our son. And I just hated it how the teachers stood around smoking tonight."

"It doesn't seem right, Betty, to send our children to school to be taught by people who don't love the Lord," Lester shared. "Oh, how I wish there were a Christian day school for them to go to, but the nearest one is 100 miles away. Hon, we must pray. Maybe the Lord wants us to start a Christian school here."

The desire to have a Christian school for his children grew in Lester's heart. Betty shared his vision. Each morning they sang and read Scriptures with their children, then sent them off to school to be educated by the world. It did not feel right. Together, they continued to pray for a Christian school, a school that would have teachers who loved the Lord and His Word.

Sometime later, Lester was the evangelist at revival meetings in Lancaster, Pennsylvania. Before he went back home, he shared with the church his desire for a private church school. He asked the people to pray about this need.

Five days later, Betty got a phone call that left her excited and praising God. "This is Virgina Mumaw," a sweet voice said. "I was in the audience the night Lester spoke of your need for a Christian day school. I am a teacher, and there are plenty of teachers here in Lancaster. I felt led by God to give you a call and let you know I would be willing to come and teach. I believe I also could get one more teacher."

Betty was overjoyed and could hardly wait to share the good news with Lester.

Some people encouraged Lester in his vision for a school; others told him it could not be done. When springtime came, Lester felt ready to call a meeting. He invited friends from other churches in the area. Russel Bear, a bishop from Lancaster, was there too. He shared the vision. Russel told Lester and the audience, "Don't hurry in planning for a school. Vote 'yes' if you are behind this project in prayer and would send your children."

Previously it had been decided that 12 votes were needed to go ahead with plans for a school. At the meeting, a basket was sent around for people to drop their votes into. While they were voting, a couple came in late. Les took time to explain to them what they were voting about. The couple later told Les, "We were so glad you didn't vote earlier. We voted 'yes.' There were exactly 12 votes!

That was in April. By fall of the next school year, a new school was ready to open its doors for 58 eager students. The following year, there were over 100. Ben Lapp generously donated land for the school. Galen Groff, Virginia

Mumaw, and Mim Musser were the first teachers. Lester Miller was the school administrator, and a faithful school board of godly men helped with the work and the many details.

One evening before school was opened, the board met in Lester's basement. That night they hoped to decide on a name.

Betty was upstairs reading stories to their four children. Lester had talked with her earlier about a name. All of a sudden *Maranatha* came to her mind. *Maranatha Christian Day School*. She wrote it on a slip of paper and asked Wendell to quietly take it down to his daddy.

Later, the children were all asleep when Lester came up and told Betty. "The name is Maranatha. There were other suggestions, but the vote for Maranatha Christian Day School was unanimous!"

Maranatha means the "the King is coming." Lester and Betty rejoiced and praised God! They prayed that their school would be the means to help neighborhood children—many, many children—to be ready when Jesus comes.

Cumberland County had its first Christian day school!

read and consider...

Of what did Lester and Betty do a great deal before they called a meeting about starting a school?

Why did they want a Christian school for their children?

What does "Maranatha" mean?

Read 2 Timothy 3:14, 15.

Proverbs 29:18: "Where there is no vision, the people perish: but he that keepeth the law, happy is he."

The Sweetest Name

There was a doctor in China who made it his practice to tell the good news of the Gospel story to all who came to his medical clinic for help. Before he treated them, he told them about Jesus Christ, the one who came to love and save all mankind.

The doctor came out to the compound early one morning before the clinic's doors were opened. Many people, plus a very old woman stooped with age, were waiting there for him. Dust clung to her clothing, feet, and sandals. The doctor could tell the old woman had come a very long way for help. He took time that morning to tell the old lady and the others the wonderful story of Jesus. The woman was so attentive to the message that he knew this story of love was touching her heart. Even as the warm rays of sunshine open the rosebud, so her heart was opening to receive the one who loved her and gave His life for her. Tears ran down her dusty cheeks.

After sharing the story of Jesus, the doctor's time was filled with attending the needs of the many people who longed for health and healing.

One morning, many weeks later, there was a knock at the busy doctor's door. Upon opening it, he found himself looking into the face of the old woman he had helped and told about Jesus weeks before. He asked her what he could do for her?

Her reply was, "Sir, He has saved me. He has made my life so happy, and I know He lives in my heart. But sir, I have forgotten His name. Could you please tell me His name again?"

The kind doctor repeated the matchless name of Jesus over and over again into the ears of the wrinkled old woman. As he repeated the name of Jesus, she too responded, "Jesus, Jesus, Jesus." Bowing low in Oriental fashion, she thanked the physician and headed back toward her village. He watched her disappear in the distance and felt a sweet assurance that never again would the woman forget the precious name of Jesus.

When Lela Long heard the story of the old woman who longed to know the name of the one who saved her and made her happy, she was inspired to write these lovely words.

Jesus is the sweetest name I know.
And He's just the same as His lovely name,
And that's the reason why I love Him so;
Oh, Jesus is the sweetest name I know.

read and consider...

Why did the old lady come to the doctor?
What did the doctor do to touch her heart for God?

Read: Psalm 145:1, 2.
Psalm 44:20, 21: "If we have forgotten the name of our God, or stretched out our hands to a strange god; shall not God search this out? for he knoweth the secrets of the heart."

chapter eleven

Good Manners

Time

Lots of time for lots of things
Though it seems that time has wings
There is always time to find
Ways of being sweet and kind;
There is always time to share
Smiles and goodness everywhere
Time to send the frowns away
Time a gentle word to say
Time for thankfulness and time
To assist the weak to climb;
Time to give a little flower,
Time for friendship, any hour.
But there is little time to spare
For unkindness anywhere.

—Author Unknown

A favorite poem of my Grandpa, Stephen R. Stoltzfus

Do Your Habits Bless Others?

Be Sweet

A little girl told her grandma, "I wouldn't mind being an old lady if I could be a sweet grandma like you."

Her grandmother wisely responded, "To be a sweet grandma start now by being a sweet little girl." This grandma had learned the lesson of being sweet and thankful. Being with her meant being refreshed and encouraged.

Be Thankful

Some people brighten a room when they come in, but thankless and complaining people brighten the room when they leave.

A minister and a rich couple were traveling. The minister asked the couple about their occupation. The man replied, "My wife is in the manufacturing business. She manufactures unhappiness."

Oh what a shame! A person who has forgotten to be thankful has fallen asleep in life! Time spent with ungrateful people seems to drain the energy right out of you, and when you leave them, you feel troubled.

There was a farmer who was known to be a complainer. He always looked on the dark side of life. One year he was blessed with an exceptionally bountiful harvest. When a friend commented on the tremendous yields, he responded with, "Yes, but a good harvest is hard on the soil."

Another ungrateful farmer did not want to acknowledge that a good harvest is a blessing from God. He said, "Imagine how my field would look if only God took care of it!" (He thought it would be full of weeds!)

Why didn't he stop and consider that his field would have been a barren wasteland if God had not sent the sunshine and the rain?

It is not a life of prosperity and ease that makes one thankful. Thankfulness comes from a heart that is filled with God.

Be Helpful

A group of kind folks from Iowa went to Arkansas for clean-up week at Calvary Bible School. Vina, a 79-year-old widow, went along to help with the cooking.

Her children said, "Mom, you are too old to go and work like that."

Vina replied, "I can work all day at home, so why shouldn't I help out?" She enjoyed cooking delicious food for the workers and was blessed by being needed and useful.

read and consider...

Are you working at developing good habits in your life? Be sweet, be thankful, and be helpful today!

Read Philippians 4:4–8.
1 Thessalonians 5:16–18: "Rejoice evermore. Pray without ceasing. In everything give thanks: for this is the will of God in Christ Jesus concerning you."

Courtesy to All

"The lady behind the counter at the post office was so friendly, courteous and helpful," Mary Ann related to her family. "She made me feel as if she were waiting all day just to see me!

"An unshaved man with a limp T-shirt, wearing shorts, came in next. I listened and watched to see how she would respond to him," Mary Ann continued.

"Hi," the lady said in a very friendly tone, "what can I do for you today?"

"I need a stamp," the unkempt man said.

"Just one?" the kind lady inquired.

Mary Ann was challenged by the postal worker's unqualified kindness to all she met. Are all people, especially your family, feeling warmth, friendliness, and courtesy from you? Other than personal appearance, speech is one of the first defining aspects of one's character. Guard your speech with all diligence.

I was at a sewing circle with my three small boys. A little girl was struggling to push open the big heavy door so she could go out. My four-year-old son, Marcellus, saw her and walked over and pushed the door open in such a manly way. Wow, I was impressed—he looked like a perfect little gentleman. I complimented him and told him I wanted to tell his daddy.

"I forgot to tell your dad!" I told my son a few days later. He said, "Well, do!" We found Mark, and I reported how Marcellus opened the door for a little girl. He stood there grinning from ear to ear.

Keep on the lookout for opportunities to show kindness.

Two Important Habits

Habits are hard to break, aren't they? Why not make some habits that you don't need to break? Something as simple as giving bananas.

Mary Mullet had a friend who came to visit her and her mother and always brought them bananas. Just bananas, but it meant so much to Mary and her mom. Make it a habit to give. If you are prompted to give something, give it. Don't think, "What would they want with that?"

My mother loves to give. Wherever she goes, she loves to take a gift along. I thought it unusual, though, when I took her to the doctor and she took a turnip out of her purse and handed it to the receptionist. "Thank you, Mrs. Stoltzfus," the receptionist so graciously said.

Who knows, maybe the receptionist's day was brightened by receiving an unusual gift.

Another good habit to develop is to acknowledge it when someone sends you a gift. Call and say thank you or send them a thank you card!

Praying is one of the most important habits you can form.

When Mark was a young boy, he got up at 5:00 to bring in the cows for milking. Every morning when he came downstairs, he would find his dad and his older brothers on their knees in the living room. He too quietly slipped to his knees. Each one prayed silently before going out to meet the day. Mark treasures that lovely memory of his dad on his knees. What an example he left to his sons!

Daily prayers give us strength for daily troubles.

A little girl in Sunday school class related, "I had a really bad sore throat. My mom prayed for me and my sore throat went away!

Another small lass said, "I had a bad sore throat, and my mom took me to the doctor. I got well too."

The wise Sunday school teacher said, "God answers prayer. God can work through medicines too and quite likely your mother prayed for you, even if you didn't know it."

Do you pray about things like sore throats? You don't need to wait for your mother to pray for you! Get in the habit of taking all your problems to God.

read and consider...

Can you brighten someone's day with a little giving?
Before you left your room this morning, did you think to pray?

Read: 2 Corinthians 9:7 and Matthew 26:41.
1 Timothy 2:8: "I will therefore that men pray everywhere, lifting up holy hands without wrath and doubting."

Brighten the Day
With Thanks and Giving

How do children learn to be thankful?

Have you learned to be thankful because you have parents who are counting their blessings? You are fortunate if you live with thankful people.

When we sit down around a table full of good food, I am grateful. Often, I will say, "I am so thankful for this food." Sometimes I will also comment that there are poor people who don't have enough to eat. I did not realize how often I said this until one day when I again said, "I am thankful for our food," two-year-old Micah in his high chair piped up, "Poor people don't have any."

Another day, my four-year-old shut off the kitchen timer for me. "You should say thank you, Mom," he called out.

Children who think of others experience more happiness and joy. It is the same for mothers who take time to reach out.

My friend Liz told me about a time when her family was talking about Thanksgiving. Her little girls wondered, "Is that when we get gifts?"

"No, dears," Liz replied, "Thanksgiving is when we should be extra thankful for all that God has given us. It is also the time when our church ladies get together and fix plates and grocery boxes for the widows and others who may be discouraged and lonely. Girls, you can go with me this year to fix the plates. First, though, you can help me make cookies. Then, when the plates are done, Dad will take all of us along to bring some cheer and sunshine to others."

I have fond memories of my mother making time for us to help fix Christmas bundles when I was a child. We each had a large new towel. We greatly enjoyed folding clothes neatly, placing them on the towel along with other useful items and a toy. Then we would wrap all in the towel and pin it shut with safety pins. Our hearts were happy, knowing we were reaching out to poor children.

There are many projects families can do to help children find joy in giving. Our children are delighted when they can go along to shop for items for Christmas bundles, school or health kits, or the Christmas shoe box project.

When we think of and do things for others, our hearts are warmly blessed. We realize anew the truth of Jesus words, "It is more blessed to give than to receive."

read and consider...

What is something your family could do to help someone in need?

Have you ever brightened the day for a widow in your church?

Read: I Timothy 6:17, 18 and Matthew 10:8.

Psalm 96:8: "Give unto the LORD the glory due unto His name: bring an offering, and come into

Pay Up!

"Owe no man anything," preached Brother Paul. I don't believe that means you cannot borrow money, but it does mean that when you borrow and your payment is due, you are under obligation to pay. If you cannot make your payment at the time specified, go and make satisfaction. Owe no man anything but to love one another. We owe a debt of love to everyone. We can never get finished paying the debt of love.

"When my wife and I were young," Paul related, "I did not have enough money to meet my bank payments one month. This weighed heavily on me. I went to the bank and told the banker, 'I am at your mercy. I don't have enough to meet this month's payment.'

"The banker appreciated my visit immensely. He told me, 'You are the first man who ever came in to tell me you could not make your payment. I will extend your loan for another month.' I walked out of the bank feeling much better than I had when I walked in. It always pays to do your best to be honest," Paul said.

read and consider...

What should a man do if he cannot make a payment?
Should a man work hard to provide the needs of his family?

Read Romans 13:8 and 2 Corinthians 8:21.
Romans 12:17: "Provide things honest in the sight of all men."

Any Spare Beds?

Most American families have a spare bed or two in the house—nice, soft beds with fluffy pillows and warm blankets.

There are many people in the world who would be happy to have just a mat to sleep on.

What is your bed like? Do you have a big wide one to roll around on? Do you share a bunk bed? Perhaps you even have a special bed, shaped like a car. Whatever you have, I doubt that it's a gunny sack!

Tim Yoder, a missionary in Kenya, Africa, said a lady in his church had been sleeping on a gunny sack on the floor for 30 years. Recently, she got her very first foam mattress to sleep on.

In Haiti, missionary Wilma Yoder visited an old lady. The old lady asked if she couldn't have some plastic bags to put on the roof so the water wouldn't come in when it rains. The inside of her house was damp and wet. Her bed was only slats across two boards with no padding on them.

God, help us to be content and thankful for what we have. We have so much!

read and consider...

What can we do to become more thankful and content? Why do we have so many blessings?

Read: Philippians 4:11, 19.
Psalm 9:2: "I will be glad and rejoice in thee: I will sing praises to thy name, O thou most High."

Disappearing Dogs!

Do you have any pet dogs at your house? What kind of dog do you have? Do you have any ankle biters?"

This is what Jim Weaver once asked the children who were in front of our church for children's class. And then he told them a story about his pet and his neighbor's wolf dog.

"Mindy, Mindy," Jim stood at the door calling his pet Pomeranian. "Mindy, Mindy, come Mindy. Mindy, where are you?"

Jim and Edith had returned late from a meeting at church. As usual, Mindy had met them at the door. Fondly they caressed their small pet. She wanted to go out. When they let her out, she was usually soon back at the door. Obviously, Mindy liked being a house dog.

Tonight was different; Mindy did not come back. Jim called her again, but Mindy did not return.

Jim and Edith lived in a development with neighbors all around them. The man who lived behind them had a wolf dog in a kennel. Sage was 97 percent wolf and 3 percent dog. He looked like a wolf! It was interesting for Jim to look out his back door and see that dog. Sage was a topic of conversation when they had visitors.

One Saturday, Sage had been loose. Jim's grandson had been at his house that day. Jim saw his little grandson wander toward the wolf dog. Quickly Jim took him indoors. He didn't know of any problems with Sage, but he didn't want to take any chances.

Now, even though it was late, Jim and his wife decided to go out with flashlights and search for Mindy. Jim went behind the house calling and looking. His wife was out front. They saw no sign of their pet. Jim went back inside. He was tired, maybe the dog would be back by morning.

"Jimmy, Jimmy," he heard Edith calling to him from behind the house. He went back out.

"Look back there, Jim; see, Sage is loose. He has something in his mouth and is shaking it. I wonder if he got Mindy? Oh, Jim, what should we do?" Edith quavered.

Quickly Jim walked over and knocked at his neighbor's front door. The man opened the door and Jim told him he thought his dog got Mindy.

"Come in," the man told Jim. "Quick, come in, it isn't safe for you to be out there if Sage is loose! Your wife will have to drive over and get you."

Jim called Edith. She drove over in their truck, way up close to the house.

"Now wait," the neighbor man said, "you have to wait till it is safe to go out."

The men stood, peering out into the dark front lawn. Pretty soon Sage came trotting around the house. Sure enough, Mindy was in his mouth! Sage dropped Mindy right beside the truck and disappeared in the darkness of the neighbor's yard.

"Now I'm leaving," Jim stated. "I'll take my dog along."

"Oh no," the neighbor said. "Just leave it there."

Jim put Mindy on the back of his truck, and the Weavers drove home. He didn't know why the man had not wanted him to take his dead dog. Did he think it would make Sage mad? Sadly, they held Mindy's mangled little body. Why, oh why did the neighbor have such a dangerous dog?

The next morning they called another neighbor and told him what had happened. They found out that this neighbor's small dog had disappeared during the night. Something had pulled it right off of his chain! Later they found it under a bush in the wolf dog's yard. They also learned that recently Sage had chased another neighbor into his garage.

They decided they'd better report this threatening wolf dog to the police.

The neighbor was fined for having a wild wolf dog without a permit. Sage was removed to a wildlife refuge.

Jim kept thinking of the words, "Love your neighbor, love your neighbor, love your neighbor."

With the help of God that is what he had tried to do.

There is always something to be thankful for. The Weavers were most grateful that Sage had not harmed their grandson and that God had kept them safe that night.

read and consider...

How do you think the Weaver's could show that they still loved their neighbor?

Do you think God could help you be kind, even if someone had taken your favorite pet?

Read: Matthew 5:43–48.

James 2:8: "If ye fulfill the royal law according to the scripture, Thou shalt love thy neighbor as thyself, ye do well."

chapter twelve

The Mighty Power of God

Precious in His Sight

Drifting, falling, gently landing,
On the coat of one child standing,
On a winter moonlit night,
Snowflakes dancing in the light.

Watching closely as they lay,
She stood in awe of what God made.
Each a masterpiece so small,
Yet the Lord sees each one fall.

Delicate and formed with love,
A gift to us from God above,
He takes the time to make each one,
For His pleasure, for our fun.

If He should care enough to make,
Each and every little flake,
Then how precious in His sight,
Is one child standing in the light.

— Author Unknown

The Blackest Three Hours

They crucified my Savior and nailed him to the cross...
Our Savior hung on that terrible tree,
Suffering shamefully for you and me...

They crucified Jesus. Then the heartless people threw more horrible darts his way, the cruel darts of unkind, mocking words.

"Save yourself, come down from the cross."

They crucified Him, then they sat down to watch Him die. The sinless Savior whose days had been filled with deeds of love and compassion to anyone in need now hung on the rugged cross, watched by the cold, hard eyes of sinful men.

Others passing by reviled and railed on him, wagging their heads. "Ah, you who said you could destroy the temple and build it in three days, save yourself. If you truly are the Son of God, come down from the cross!"

Scribes, elders, and priests mocked him, "He saved others; himself He cannot save. If he be the King of Israel, let Him now come down from the cross and we will believe Him."

To all of these darts Jesus' heart cry was the most gracious and compassionate, "Father, forgive them, for they know not what they do."

One of the thieves who was crucified with Jesus jeered at him, "If thou be the Christ, save thyself and us."

Then, as a ray of light in this dark hour, the other thief rebuked him, saying, "Dost thou not fear God, seeing thou art in the same condemnation? We receive the due reward of our deeds, but this man hath done nothing amiss." Then he said to Jesus, "Lord, remember me when thou comest into thy kingdom."

"Today, thou shalt be with me in paradise," Jesus replied, with love and forgiveness in His eyes.

God silenced the tongues of the wicked watchers by darkening the sun. Darkness, an eerie, thick black pall hung over all Creation as the Creator hung on the old rugged cross. From 12 noon to 3 p.m., darkness covered all the earth, and then as He died, He cried, "Father, into thy hands I commend my spirit."

A great earthquake shook the ground, huge rocks split apart. The veil in the temple was rent. Graves were opened, many bodies of the saints which slept arose.

The centurion who stood by the cross said, "Certainly, this was a righteous man; without a doubt, the Son of God!"

What a wonderful, wonderful Savior, to die on the cross for me. My soul is thrilled, my heart is filled, to think— He died for me.

"He could have called ten thousand angels to destroy the world and set Him free. He could have called ten thousand angels, but He died alone for you and me."

read and consider...

Jesus' Example

What did Jesus say when He was mocked?
What did He say when He was misunderstood, rejected and
   dying?
What were the last words He uttered before He died?

The seven sayings of the cross:

1. "Father, forgive them, for they know not what they do."
2. "Verily, verily I say unto thee, today thou shalt be with me in Paradise."
3. "Woman, behold thy son!" "Behold thy mother."
4. "I thirst."
5. "My God, my God why hast thou forsaken me?"
6. "It is finished."
7. "Father, into thy hands I commend my spirit."

Ten Thousand Angels by Ray Overholt, 1958.

read and consider...

Each one of us needs to consider the words we speak.
Someday we will give account to God.
He has a record of all our words!

Read Mark 15:25–29.
Matthew 27:54: "Now when the centurion, and they that were with him, watching Jesus, saw the earthquake and those things that were done, they feared greatly, saying, Truly this was the Son of God."

Oh, Yes, I've Been Changed

Jesus not only has power over nature and animals, *He has all power*. Even the demons tremble and bow before Him.

Imagine the terrible plight of a man possessed by the devil. The man was so fierce and strong that even chains could not hold him. He wore no clothes. He lived in the tombs, where he could be heard crying. You can be certain that that was a most eerie sound. This man cut himself with rocks. He was unkempt and looked terrible. No one could tame him or control him. He had no human friend.

Yet there was a friend who cared and knew all about his sad plight. One day, Jesus and His disciples came to the country of the Gadarenes. When the possessed man saw Jesus, he ran to Him. Falling down before Jesus, he worshiped and cried out with a loud voice, "What have I to do with Thee Jesus, thou Son of God Most High?"

Jesus commanded the unclean spirit to come out of the man. Jesus asked the spirit, "What is thy name?"

He replied, "Legion, for we are many." Then these evil spirits begged Jesus to send them into a nearby herd of swine.

Jesus told them, "Go."

Imagine the shock and terror of the keepers of the swine when suddenly the pigs became possessed. The two thousand swine ran violently down a steep place and plunged to their death in the sea.

The men responsible for the swine ran too. They fled to the city and told their shocking tale. The whole city streamed out to see what had been done.

There was not a pig to be seen, but the man out of whom the devils were cast was sitting calmly at the feet of Jesus, clothed and in his right mind.

The people were filled with fear. They begged Jesus to leave their region.

The changed man wanted to go with Jesus. But Jesus told him, "Go home to your own house and friends. Show them what great things God did for you. Tell of His wonderful compassion."

The man who was healed became a wonderful missionary. He proclaimed throughout the whole city the great things God had done to him.

Later, when Jesus returned, the people gladly received Him. They were all waiting for His return.

read and consider...

Why did Jesus allow the evil spirits to go into the swine?
Did he do this to get the people's attention?
Jesus still changes men's lives today.

Read Luke 8:39, 40.
Matthew 28:18: "All power is given unto me in heaven and in earth."

Lord of the Storm

"Oh," said Jenny at church on Sunday, "I just positively dread Thursday night."

"Whatever could be so bad?" wondered her dear friend Sara.

Thursday is the night the motorcycle gangs meet in the field across the road from us," Jenny Wheatley wailed. "Their music is loud and terrible. I won't be able to sleep a wink."

"Well, Jenny, let's pray about it," Sara said. The two girls bowed their heads. "Dear Father," Sara prayed, "please intervene. We know these motorcycle gangs and their music are not pleasing to You. Lord, we give you our cares and worries. We ask for your protection and peace for Thursday night. Please give Jenny rest and sleep. Amen."

Thursday dawned clear and sunny. Hundreds of motorcyclists pulled into the grassy field across from the Wheatley's. Jenny was sad as she watched them pour into her neighborhood. They set up their grandstand. As twilight fell, the drums began to beat, louder and louder, until they reverberated throughout the area.

This was no ordinary music—it was hard rock, pleasing to the devil and his demons.

The music was well underway when dark storm clouds began to roll in. The music of God Almighty's thunder and jagged streaks of lightning cut through the night. The rain poured down in torrents. The terrific thunderstorm kept on, hour after hour. The storm completely drowned out the wild party. The next morning, the wet and miserable motorcycle gangs left.

To appreciate the wonder of this miraculous storm, you must understand that thunderstorms are rare in Ireland. A missionary who lives near the Wheatley's said, "In our six years in Ireland, we have never had a storm close to one like this. Was it merely a coincidence that such an unusual storm came to this exact area at precisely the right time? Was this not an answer to the women's prayers? What a wonderful confirmation of the amazing love and power of our great God.

Resource: The MIC newsletter, June-July, 2002.

read and consider...

When you are worried and troubled, what do you do? Does it help to share your care with other Christians?

Read Psalm 56:3 and James 5:16–18.
1 Peter 5:7: "Casting all your care upon him; for he careth for you."

Water Miracles

You may have just taken a cool drink of water. Did you know that water is miracle material? God used water many times in miracles and to teach lessons about Himself.

In the Old Testament, Pharaoh would not let the children of Israel go as Moses requested. God sent a most unusual punishment. Moses smote the waters of the Nile River with his rod, and the waters turned to red blood. The fish died, and that awful red water stank. The Egyptians could not drink it.

Finally, after ten terrible plagues, Pharaoh told Moses to go. But when his heart was hardened, he pursued the children of Israel with a mighty army. The Israelites were sore afraid and cried unto the Lord. God miraculously saved them by making a dry path through the Red Sea. The waters stood in a wall on either side of this Red Sea road. When the Egyptians followed on this amazing path, God told Moses to stretch out his hand over the sea, and the waters returned, covering all the host of Pharaoh.

The mighty waters of the Red Sea obeyed the voice of God Almighty!

As the children of Israel journeyed through the wilderness, they were in desperate need of water. They were overjoyed to find water at Marah. But those who drank, spat it out, for it was bitter.

"What shall we drink?" the people murmured. The Lord showed Moses a tree to throw into the water and the water became sweet.

Later, water was scarce again. The people demanded that Moses give them water! "Why were we brought out of Egypt to be killed by thirst?" they complained. They even contemplated stoning Moses. But Moses knew where to go. He cried out to God. God told Moses to smite a rock at Horeb. Water gushed out in abundance.

In the New Testament, Jesus turned water into wine. He walked on water. He calmed the stormy Sea of Galilee with his power-filled words, "Peace, be still."

The next time you take a drink of water, let it remind you of the mighty God we serve!

read and consider...

Can you recall more miraculous water stories?
Do you know Jesus, the Living Water?

Read John 4:10, 14.
Luke 8:25: "What manner of man is this! For he commandeth even the winds and water, and they obey him."

Disgusting Delays

Verda smiled with satisfaction as she zipped her suit-
case shut. Today was the day she had been anticipating
for weeks. "Finally Karen and I are flying back to Pennsylvania to visit my dear precious Mama," Verda mused.
"Dear Mama, already 94 years old, but so alert and loving.
Oh, I am so anxious to be with her again."

"Karen," Verda called, "Are you ready to leave?"
"Yes, Mama, everything is packed and ready."

"Oh, Karen," Verda sighed as she glanced out the
window, "Look, there is Tomas, likely coming to buy eggs.
Oh, he can be so talkative." Eli went out to wait on Tomas.
The minutes ticked by as the men chatted and Verda fret-
ted. It was time to leave for the airport. Verda went out,
started their little blue car, turned it around and loaded
everything. She felt like hollering for Eli to come. "Maybe
he'll at least get the hint that we're ready now," she
hoped.

Finally Tomas left. Eli, Verda, and Karen were soon
zooming down the road. Verda sighed as she settled in
her seat. Her mind was full of her family in Pennsylvania.
She had truly left Father and Mother when she married Eli
years ago. They had lived in El Salvador ever since their
wedding.

They were traveling along for 30 or more minutes
when Verda's reverie was abruptly interrupted. Suddenly
their car was shaking from side to side. Eli gripped the
wheel tightly. "Do I have a flat?" he wondered. But then
the car shook up and down. Eli fought to keep control

of the wheel, slowing down and stopping as soon as he could. "It's an earthquake!" Karen hollered. "Thank you, God, for keeping us safe," Eli rejoiced. Others were not as fortunate. A van traveling the same route had crashed into a tree. They saw great clouds of dust rising from the mountains up ahead.

Eli and Verda did not realize that El Salvador had just been struck by a major earthquake. They had no idea the extent of the disaster that was taking place. Farther along, the road was blocked. They detoured to another route leading to the airport, keeping a sharp watch for poles, branches, or boulders that had fallen on the road.

Verda was grateful when they finally pulled into the airport. But alas, it was shut down. The quake had hit here too. Runways were cracked and buckled. There was nothing to do now but go back home.

Later that day, Eli and Verda learned that the Pan American Highway they had been traveling on that morning had suffered massive landslides. Tons and tons of earth had rushed down the mountainsides, burying vehicles and people in its path. This earthquake on January 13, 2001, had caused terrible devastation and loss of life.

It was dark when Eli and Verda reached home. They had been so concerned. Were their children all safe? What a comfort to see their sons come out the door. What a joy to feel their love and warm embraces. Their house, too, was not in shambles. All that was broken was a mirror, two jars, and a vase.

Verda felt so humbled and overwhelmed with gratitude to God for His protection. "Just think, if neighbor

Tomas had not kept us waiting this morning, we might have been buried in those awful landslides."

"Oh, God," Verda breathed, "I want to be more trusting and patient."

Down Like Dominos

The morning of July 10, 1976, was warm and overcast. A real storm was brewing. Lightning streaked its jagged forks across the sky. Thunder crashed and echoed through the hills and hollows in eastern Ohio.

Mark and his brothers and sisters had all hurried to the house when they saw the storm approaching. They stood in awe at God's power revealed in the storm as the rain came down in torrents.

Suddenly, there was an extra brilliant lightning streak. Mom gasped as she saw it strike a large ash tree in the meadow behind the house. The milk cows had taken shelter under that very tree. It was raining so hard that the Beachy family could not see far as they anxiously peered out the window. It appeared as if some of the cows were injured.

When the rain subsided, Mark ran out to the pasture to check on the cattle. Twenty of them had fallen over; dead cows lay like dominos, so close they had fallen on each other. The cows that were left walked nervously about. Mark could hardly believe his eyes!

There were only 39 cows in the herd and now over half had been struck dead. What a powerful lightning bolt! Mark raced back to the house to tell the rest of his family.

In his journal that night, Mark wrote about the days' events. He included his own testimony. "God is good, we are all alive."

Mark also remembers what his dad said in church the next day. He briefly related what had happened to his cattle in the storm and stated that he can say with Job, "The LORD gave, and the LORD hath taken away; blessed be the name of the LORD" (Job 1:21).

read and consider...

How can we praise God through difficult days?

Can we see the handiwork of God in nature and in storms?

Did you know Psalm 104:3 says that God makes the clouds His chariot, and He walks on the wings of the wind?

Read: Isaiah 25:1–4.

Psalm 148:7, 8: "Praise the LORD from the earth, ye dragons, and all deeps: fire, and hail; snow, and vapor; stormy wind fulfilling his word."

Rescued at the Brink

A 48-year-old man lost a large sum of money by gambling. This so discouraged him that he felt life was not worth living. He decided to end his life on March 19, 2003. He went to the Niagara River rapids and walked past the safety lines and signs.

To him death looked more inviting than life. But death without Christ is the most awful state a man can be in. Yet, at Niagara Falls there is one suicide monthly and many more attempts.

The man took off his cap and wallet and placed them on the ice. A note he placed in his cap said, "Tell my parents that I am sorry."

He slid down an icy slope, plunging into the Niagara River. He ended up 20 feet from the shore and five feet from the edge of the Horseshoe Falls. There, he desperately held his footing in the icy water for two hours. The 170 foot drop to the roiling base of the falls now struck terror into his heart.

A rescue team rushed to the scene. One fireman commented, "God is just holding him there."

Police officers and city firefighters in insulated suits waded into the river in hopes of reaching the man, but the current and the ice prevented them from rescuing him.

The Erie County Sheriff's Department sent out a helicopter which hovered over the man, but the wind and the currents blew the rescue ring they dropped away from him.

The man cried out, "Help! Help! I can't hold on much longer."

One more step, and he would have been hurled into eternity.

"Hurry," the man hoarsely yelled, "I'm losing my hold."

Rescue workers standing on Terrapin Point held onto ropes attached to the ring dropped from the helicopter. Then the ring was finally dropped within reach of the desperate man. He lunged forward and desperately grabbed the life ring.

The rescue workers who pulled him out of the icy waters said they had never before saved someone who was so close to the brink. It was the most dramatic falls rescue in their memory.

At the hospital, the man said he didn't know what he would have done had someone lost his life in an attempt to save him.

Did anyone point this despondent man to Jesus, the One who gave His life to save the souls of all men? God's power and love are strong enough to change any life and give purpose and meaning to our days.

read and consider...

What brink are you standing on?
What are you doing to help those who have the waves of
    despair crashing down around them?
Who alone can satisfy your soul and give meaning to your life?
Read: Psalm 94:17, 18 and Psalm 119:116, 117.
John 3:16: "For God so loved the world, that he gave his only
    begotten Son, that whosoever believeth in him should not
    perish, but have everlasting life."

Frogs and Fish Listen

Oh God of awesome power and might,
We bow before your name each night.
You see the tiny sparrow fall,
You're the Maker, Monarch, and Savior of all!

The animal kingdom obeys your will,
The waters hearken when you say, "Peace be still."
You shut the lions' mouths and opened the bears',
You know the minute number of our hairs.

Oh God of awesome power and might,
We bow before your name each night.
　　　　　　　　　—Mary Ellen Beachy

The animal kingdom pays a tribute of honor to God by obeying His commands.

Think of the angel shutting the lions' mouths when Daniel was thrown into their den. Those lions were very hungry, but they could not touch Daniel.

Do you wish you had been an Egyptian child when God punished Pharaoh by sending the plague of frogs? God told the frogs to come up out of the river. They came in abundance; likely there were millions of hopping green frogs. The houses were full of frogs. Frogs were even in their beds. Frogs were in the kitchen where they kneaded bread, and frogs were in their ovens. (Anyone care for a baked frog?) Frogs were on the people, too. Do you think it was hard to rest and sleep with so many frogs around?

You can be thankful you were not with that naughty group of youth who mocked the prophet Elisha many long years ago. They said to him, "Go up thou bald head, go up thou bald head." Elisha cursed them, or called for judgment upon them.

Who do you think sent those two fierce mama bears out of the woods? Those bears gave 42 youth a most awful punishment. Imagine how horrible it would be to be torn by a bear!

Remember the run-away prophet Jonah? God sent a mighty storm to stop Jonah. Then Jonah was thrown overboard. God prepared that great big fish to swallow up and save Jonah. That fish ride was a dramatic lesson on obedience.

On another day, 153 fish obeyed God too. The disciples were fishing all night and caught nothing. Jesus came on the scene and told them to cast down their net on the other side of the boat. They obeyed and miraculously caught many fish. Their nets were nearly breaking. Peter cried out, "It is the Lord!"

Are you listening when God speaks to you?

Can you recall other accounts in Scripture where animals and nature obeyed their maker God?

read and consider...

Read John 21:3-7 and 2 Kings 2:23, 24 in the *Amplified Bible*.
Psalm 104:24: "O Lord, how manifold are thy works! In wisdom
    hast thou made them all: the earth is full of thy riches."
Job 12:7-10: "But ask now the beasts, and they shall teach
    thee; and the fowls of the air, and they shall tell thee: or
    speak to the earth, and it shall teach thee; and the fishes
    of the sea shall declare unto thee. Who knoweth not in all
    these things that the hand of the LORD hath wrought this?
    In whose hand is the soul of every living thing, and the
    breath of all mankind."

Did You Enjoy

The Horse That Worked for God?

Don't miss Mary Ellen Beachy's other children's book;
Light For Your Path...

Light for Your Path
Paperback
235 pages
$10.99
Item #LIG76105

A wonderful children's book has been updated and revised! *Light for Your Path*, is a devotional of short stories for young readers. This book is ideal reading for children in devotional times. The stories bring the practicality of God's Word into everyday situations. Character traits such as honesty, meekness, obedience, serving others, willingness, and diligence are brought into focus to leave an impression on young minds.

At the end of each story is a treasure search of Bible verses that are relevant to the story's message.

More Children's Books!

Welcome to an exciting new series of books from Vision Publishers aimed at helping children adjust to changes in life!

As children grow, they are bound to discover that life inevitably brings changes. These changes can be unsettling experiences to young children, but they can also be stepping stones as they look back and see parental love and God's faithfulness through all of life.

We Build a House
Hardcover - 24 pages - Full Color - 10 x 8 - $10.99 - Item #HOU76211

In We Build a House, journey with little Adam through the experience of the family building a new house. Children will enjoy the many color pictures throughout the book, as they look at the move through the eyes of a little one. They will also see that Adam can adjust to this change because of the love and security he feels in his home.

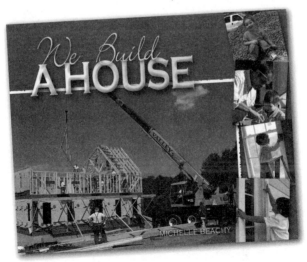

Am I My Brother's Keeper?

My Brother's Keeper

Hardcover - 24 pages - Full Color - 10 x 8 - $10.99 - Item #BRO76204

Join young Andrew Martin as he learns to adapt to life with a handicapped brother named Benjamin. Andrew discovers, as many children have, that not all changes in life are easy, but there are important lessons to be learned and to be thankful for.

I just wish Jesus still lived in Galilee. Then we could take Benjamin to see Jesus and he'd be well.

I used to pray and ask God to heal Benjamin. Then Mama told me this is God's plan for our lives. We don't know why, but God chose our family to take care of a special needs child. Now I pray that God would keep Benjamin from having a seizure while he sleeps and that He would help us take good care of Benjamin.

> - from the book

Order Form

To order, send this completed order form to:

Vision Publishers
P.O. Box 190
Harrisonburg, VA 22803
Fax: 540-437-1969
E-mail: orders@vision-publishers.com
www.vision-publishers.com

_____ _____
Name   Date

_____ _____
Mailing Address   Phone

_____
City   State   Zip

The Horse That Worked for God   Qty. _____ x $10.99 ea. = _____

Light for Your Path   Qty. _____ x $10.99 ea. = _____

My Brother's Keeper   Qty. _____ x $10.99 ea. = _____

We Build a House   Qty. _____ x $10.99 ea. = _____

(Please call for quantity discounts - 877-488-0901)

Price _____

Virginia residents add 5% sales tax _____

Ohio residents add applicable sales tax _____

Shipping & handling ___**$4.20**___

Grand Total _____

❏ Check #_____

❏ Money Order   ❏ Visa   **All Payments in US Dollars**

❏ MasterCard   ❏ Discover

Name on Card _____

Card # __|__|__|__ __|__|__|__|__ __|__|__|__|__ __|__|__|__

3-digit code from signature panel __|__|__ Exp. Date __|__|__|__

Thank you for your order!

For a complete listing of our books write for our catalog.
Bookstore inquiries welcome

Order Form

To order, send this completed order form to:

Vision Publishers
P.O. Box 190
Harrisonburg, VA 22803
Fax: 540-437-1969
E-mail: orders@vision-publishers.com
www.vision-publishers.com

_____   _____
Name   Date

_____   _____
Mailing Address   Phone

_____
City   State   Zip

The Horse That Worked for God   Qty. _____ x $10.99 ea. = _____

Light for Your Path   Qty. _____ x $10.99 ea. = _____

My Brother's Keeper   Qty. _____ x $10.99 ea. = _____

We Build a House   Qty. _____ x $10.99 ea. = _____

(Please call for quantity discounts - 877-488-0901)

Price _____

Virginia residents add 5% sales tax _____

Ohio residents add applicable sales tax _____

Shipping & handling ____ **$4.20** ____

Grand Total _____

☐ Check #_____

☐ Money Order   ☐ Visa   **All Payments in US Dollars**

☐ MasterCard   ☐ Discover

Name on Card _____

Card # __|__|__|__ __|__|__|__|__ __|__|__|__|__ __|__|__|__|__

3-digit code from signature panel __|__|__ Exp. Date __|__|__|__

Thank you for your order!

For a complete listing of our books write for our catalog.
Bookstore inquiries welcome